Arise Shine & Live

On Resilience, Faith, and Bipolar Disorder

Lisa Rumpel

Arise Shine & Live

On Resilience, Faith, and Bipolar Disorder

Copyright © 2022 Lisa Rumpel

All rights reserved. No part of this publication may be reproduced, stored in a retrieval system, or transmitted in any form or by any means electronic, mechanical, photocopying, recording or otherwise, without the prior written permission of the author.

ISBN: 9798369766408

Dedication

I dedicate this book to the memory of my cousin Michele.

And to you the reader, may you find hope to live bravely and hang on when life gets hard.

Contents

Introduction 11

1. Anxiety with my groceries 14
2. Run with hope 17
3. Praise and lament 23
4. Finding purpose out of darkness 26
5. It takes a forest to lift a spirit 31
6. Confession: a race to mercy 35
7. Healing comes in surprising ways 38
8. Whether your song is happy or sad, God is listening .. 42
9. Jesus' resurrection fuels my joy 45
10. We need the support of others 49
11. On being salty and bright 53
12. Never give up on hope 56
13. Baby Jesus brings joy to a hurting soul 59

14. Quebec churches cured my cold and loneliness ...63

15. Delicious dessert—a divine gift............................69

16. Stand by me, Lord..72

17. God wants us to be happy....................................75

18. Seasons of blues, seasons of beauty 78

19. Who are your Jedi? 81

20. Collect your blessings 85

21. Home is where God is..89

22. Resilience and resurrection in a pandemic........93

23. Hope is a muscle we need to exercise..................98

24. "Just to be alive is a grand thing"......................101

25. The joy of dancing like nobody's watching........104

26. The prayer in doing chores................................107

27. Gifts and crosses 110

28. When life goes up in smoke, keep a sense of humour, kindness, and grit 113

29. Prayer of a "silly woman in front of the tabernacle" ..117

30. Redesign your living space and unclutter your mind for Jesus.. 120

31. When your heart dips low, turn to Jesus.......... 124

32. Riches are in relationships 128

33. Walking in the garden with God....................... 132

34. Making use of therapy, sleep, and a good dose of laughter 136

35. You're not a robot 140

36. All shall be well 144

37. Choose an attitude of hope 148

38. Writing as a form of prayer and healing 152

39. Any storm can be weathered 157

40. Is seeking forgiveness your cross?..................... 160

41. Leave "if only" behind 164

42. Is connection on your "have a good day" checklist?.. 168

43. When it feels like He's not there........................172

44. Holiness is a lifelong journey 176

45. A fresh perspective.. 180

46. A chef's healing cooking 184

47. Inspired by an Italian pianist and composer ..188

48. God delights in you through all your troubles . 192

49. Even in adversity there can be joy 196
50. The bravest thing you can do is ask for help 200
　　 Acknowledgements 204
　　 Works Cited 207
　　 Resources 220
　　 About the Author 221

Foreword

"These vignettes reveal more than the trials Lisa has faced; they provide a beautiful example of her resilience that will inspire others who carry a cross to keep walking toward the resurrection. She shares vulnerably, suggests practically, and gives hope."

-Stephanie Gray Connors, Speaker and Author

"In a marketplace that spends so much time in darkness, Lisa Rumpel has written a wonderful invitation to return to the light. Through vulnerably sharing stories of the struggles she faces, steps she took and grace that guided her forward, Lisa invites the rest of us to Arise, Shine and Live, too. Read this book now and thank me later."

-John O'Leary, #1 National Best-Selling Author of the books ON FIRE and IN AWE

"In Arise, Shine, & Live, Lisa brings her reader along with her on this beautiful journey of comfort, hope, faith, pain, and joy in different waves. Her words flow and allow you to pause and reflect on your experience with your mental health and fitness. I can relate to her coping practices, and I know that I am not alone. Her incredible references shed more light on the need to hold on to hope and faith through all the experiences in life and dance with it. This is a great book and easy read for anyone who is challenged with coping with their mental health and for people who want to support their loved ones who are experiencing mental health illnesses."

-Rasie Bamigbade, Leadership Coach.Book Coach.Author.Speaker

"Inviting us into her daily experience of living with bipolar disorder, Lisa Rumpel's poignant, wonderfully told vignettes reveal that she has grasped the indescribable love and delight God has for her. Her quiet certitude that God will faithfully meet her needs, and her relentless pursuit of Him in the prayer, sacraments and community of the Church, are a beautiful example of resting in the strength of Jesus, the source of her hope. Whether engaging with nature, dancing, doing her chores, connecting with family and friends, enjoying a good meal, or watching Star Wars, Lisa's fearless determination, as a self-described "resilient Catholic," to seek out joy and to live from a place of hope is truly inspiring. Her stories of letting go of the stigma and shame of having a mental illness will bring encouragement to many."

-The Most Reverend J. Michael Miller, CSB, Archbishop of Vancouver

Introduction

Be brave, my child; the Lord of heaven and earth grant you joy in place of this sorrow of yours. Be brave, my daughter (Tobit 7:18).

Stretching for the next hold, I reached for a rock edge that protruded out and gripped my fingers tightly around it. My breath came in and out quickly. I supported my body weight by jamming my shoe in a rock crevice. My food wedged into the rock formation and my right hand grasped another above me. I looked down at my brother below as he held onto the ropes, in case of a fall. The harness cinched around my waist and was snugly wrapped around my thighs. My rock-climbing shoes were uncomfortable as they were a size smaller than normal to keep from slipping.

Beads of sweat popped up along my hairline and my armpits. I looked up and saw how much further I had to go. My muscles strained as I grasped the rocks along the crack in the large rock surface. I wedged my feet into another hold and slowly pulled my body up. My focus was completely on making my way up the mountain in Squamish—no distracting thoughts buzzed around in my head.

My brother shouted, "You are almost there! You can do it."

My breath was heavy, and my muscles were getting tired. My hamstrings were taut, and my arms ripped. I thrust my left hand out and jumped to grab the next hold. Nearing the top, my heart pounded even faster feeling the excitement of reaching the summit. A few more grunts, I pushed, pulled, and reached until I lifted my body up and over the edge. I stood carefully and took in the sight. Breathless and proud of myself, I drank in the vista of mountains meeting ocean. The sun was still shining, the dinner hour fast approaching. This successful rock-climbing trip with my older brother boosted my sense of accomplishment. I repelled back down with gusto, still feeling on top of the world.

Little did I know that in just a few years, I would need similar climbing skills to help me out of a dark place—one labeled with a mental illness that included medications, side effects, fears, stigma, and doubts about living. The determination and grit I used for climbing became essential in my recovery and helped me foster the will to thrive.

Writing these essays about my struggle with mental illness has been a battle of resistance, and it is because of many small victories that this book is now in your hands. The desire to write this book has been burning in my heart for years, and, although I had to overcome stigma to do so, it was healing to write about my experiences.

I wish to shed some light on an often dark and silent fight for health and happiness by those who live with mental illness.

If you struggle with a mental illness, know that you are not alone. Reaching out for help is one of the bravest things you can do.

May families who bring care to a family member who has a mental illness be inspired that it does get better! Through much adversity I have discovered that life is worth living and hope is worth sharing.

1. Anxiety with my groceries

I balanced a chicken, toilet paper, potatoes, and kale in my arms, while the bananas hanging from my pinky pulled at my finger, straining it. I counted seven people ahead of me in line, including a family with a cart piled high and an upset customer. My skin started to burn. My throat dried up, and my hands sweated like I had just finished an intense aerobics class. My head spun and my heartbeat as hard as a djembe in a drum circle. I was dizzy and weak. My whole body trembled. *I thought I was over this. How come this is happening to me?* I focused. Took shaky breaths and blew the air out like I was extinguishing the candles on a birthday cake. My thoughts spiralled. *I am getting sick again.* I did what I had been taught (Low).

I found a good thought to push out the negative ones. *Calm begets calm.* Another one. *It's distressing but not dangerous.*

Bear the discomfort and still function.

It was my turn to check out. I dropped my groceries on the conveyor belt and took another deep breath. My thoughts and limbs were vibrating like mad.

"Do you have a points card?"

"Yes." My voice came out breathy and quiet, as I used my energy to keep myself vertical and breathing. I dug my sweaty hand into my purse to find my cards.

"Do you want a bag?"

"Yes." My voice was stronger. I had a plan. Grab groceries. Sit in the deli. Drink water. Let the panic pass.

As soon as the cashier handed me the receipt, I walked to an empty chair in the deli. I sat stunned. After a few minutes, I remembered another way to calm down. Looking around, I found words starting with the letter "s." Using objective thinking derailed the vicious cycle of thoughts barrelling around in my mind.

I unzipped my jacket. *Sale, sandwich, salted, soup* ... My breathing slowed. *Savoury, sweet, sundried* ... My hands became cooler. My throat moistened as I sipped more water. My heartbeats steadied.

A few more minutes passed, and I felt ready to walk to the sky train and head home. The hardest part now was not to interrogate myself for reasons why I had a panic attack in the grocery store.

It came and went. I had to let it be.

Feelings and sensations rise and fall, come and go if we let them.

I picked up my groceries and left the store. Relieved. The cold air hit my face and I inhaled. *I can do this. Anxiety can't keep me down.* I walked briskly, mulling over which herbs to season the chicken with. Raindrops cooled my skin as they brushed my cheeks falling softly. With each step I could feel my muscles relaxing. I couldn't wait to cook dinner. Instead of nausea and trembling, my stomach growled with hunger.

Lights from passing cars glimmered in the puddles. People walked by me unaware of my small victory. I smiled in the fading light. *I have no control over my outer environment, only my inner one. The worst had not happened. I am not in danger. There is only peace.*

I faced panic, and now I would prepare a cozy chicken dinner at home.

Prepare your favourite meal.

2. Run with hope

The third kilometer of the five-kilometer race was the hardest. My muscles became tired and my breathing ragged. The heat was unbearable. Doubt crept in. *I should stop, I am not fit for this,* popped up in my mind. *It's too hard. My body is tired.*

With a quick decision to continue running, to finish the race, to not give up, I pushed through the pain. A surge of will rose and determination took over. *I have got to finish this race. I can do it. I want to complete it. I need to do this for me.*

I want to be a runner, an athlete. I want to be a saint. A saint is a spiritual athlete.

I run seeking the exhilaration the endorphins give me. Exercise is one of my tools for wellness. Even a short walk improves my mental state. Creativity flows and problems look smaller. My mental health flourishes when I am active.

When I walked to school along farm fields at 5 years old, I used to try and outrun cars. It became a game rother used as a tactic to get us there on time. A little older, I ran in races in the fall to win pumpkins. In grade 3, I joined track and started running longer races. I overheard my gym teacher tell my mom, "She runs like the wind!"

A few years ago, when I trained for a race in the middle of a Vancouver winter, I ran in the rain a lot. My feet would get soaked by the first splash and my legs would get wet. After that, I ran straight through the middle of puddles. It was amazing to see what I can withstand when I don't rely on my own strength but the Lord's. In St. Paul's letter to the Romans, he says, "...we rejoice in our sufferings, knowing that suffering produces endurance, and endurance produces character, and character produces hope, and hope does not disappoint us, because God's love has been poured into our hearts through the Holy Spirit that has been given to us" (Romans 5:3).

The strength I get from managing bipolar disorder increases my will to live and to live full of purpose. As a Catholic woman, I run to the source of my hope, Jesus. When I receive the sacraments, holy Mass and confession, they nourish my mind, body, and soul. Feet flying over pavement, running shoes smacking percussion over the hum of cars, my spirit soars. Running gives me a wild feeling of freedom. I am racing to my next adventure, and I am thrilled.

I didn't always have a zest for life. During my graduating year of high school, instead of joining my classmates on a weekend retreat, I took a trip to a Mental Hospital.

Sleepless nights. Yet boundless energy. My moods cycled rapidly from euphoria to depression. Despairing voices bombarded me. Characters in movies I watched gave me secret messages. Strangers stared as I offered broken pieces of chocolate to them. Deeply sad I spiralled into the depths of a dark place. Standing in front of the bathroom mirror at home, I looked at my reflection. Dark hair, red lips, pale face; I was snow white pretending to be okay. My shoulders slumped, the weight of sadness and fear knocking me down. Negative voices became louder and louder. I couldn't shut out the chatter.

You're not good enough.

Why try?

What's the point of living?

Will they really miss you?

You don't belong here.

Your family will be better off without you.

Why should I live?

Tears ran in silent streams down my face. I hid in the bathroom with the door locked, in suffocating isolation. I didn't want to end my life. I had no plan but the suicidal thoughts kept poking at me. They wouldn't leave me alone. I uttered two words.

Help me!

And somehow God triumphed. He heard my prayer.

Knocking loudly my mom unlocked the door. My sobs weren't as quiet as I thought. My mom found me crumpled on the floor. Tears were rapidly falling and streaking dark lines of makeup around my bloodshot eyes. She asked, "Are you okay?" I could barely speak. My muscles were weak and heavy.

"No." I struggled to lift myself off the floor.

Falling back down, she tenderly picked me up, handing me my fuzzy, purple and white snowflake pajamas.

Gently, with her hand on my back she ushered me into the living room. I sat at the piano slowly playing the song "Only Hope." I cried. Shaking violently, I dropped to the ground. I rocked back and forth. My mom called my dad on the phone to come home.

I shook from head to foot, crying and shouting. My mom rubbed my back in slow soothing circles. As soon as my dad arrived with the family van, my sister guided me down the stairs. Carefully walking as we shuffled down side by side. I leaned all my weight on her. My parents drove me to a hospital. A long drive from comfort. I was admitted to an adult psychiatric ward.

All the while in the car, the sound of Christmas music was playing on the radio. The whispered prayers of my parents almost escaped my notice. In the emergency room a nurse questioned me. I was given a hospital bed and sleeping pills to settle me. They didn't work.

Cold and frightened, I was on the first steps of a journey, one I hadn't planned. I was empty of hope. I felt abandoned. Where was Jesus now? I didn't feel His presence, but I know I was not alone on that scary night in November.

I needed a Saviour, a refuge, a healer. And He came searching for me. I only needed to turn to Him. I needed rescuing. Fear, anxiety, sadness, loneliness, and hopelessness were my only companions. I couldn't save myself. This was it. I could sink or swim.

I heard a small voice say, *Let go and hold on to God*. At 17 years old, I decided I would do everything I could to heal.

We don't know what good might happen the next minute, hour, month, or year. It's worth living to find out. Out of my experiences of darkness, I have become hope filled because I cling to my faith.

A saint loves the Lord by getting up again and again. Each day I will rise and do my best.

Reflect on Romans 5:1-5 in your prayer.

3. Praise and lament

Sun rays dapple the sidewalk. Evening bird calls. Summer months promise fun and relaxation. But when you have a mood disorder, happy feelings don't always fill your brain. I remember darkness seeping into my thoughts one summer night. My mood dropped like a speeding roller coaster.

Instead of reacting with self-compassion, I berated myself for feeling depressed. *Don't be silly. It's sunny. Don't feel this way. You are so weak. Why are you feeling depressed again? You're supposed to have fun.*

I headed out for a walk with hope-filled music in my earbuds. I didn't know why I was crying. I hoped no one saw the tears falling behind my sunglasses. I walked. Fading light. Chalk drawings. Lush flower beds. Dancing shadows on pavement. I focused on the present moment.

Feeling depressed can be isolating, but it's the most important time to reach out. After years of experiencing depression and mania, I'm more aware of the signs and symptoms of the mental illness I manage. My top resources for help are calling a friend or family member and praying.

Adjusting the dose of my medication with the help of my doctor is good too. Sleeping eight hours a night, eating healthy food, and exercising are essential. Sleep restores the serotonin levels in the brain. Serotonin acts like a messenger to our brain cells and helps regulate our moods, including anxiety and happiness. Even athletes recognize the importance of sleep. At ten hours they have peak performance.

For me, self-care is not optional. I pray to the Lord, praising and crying out to Him. Opening my heart with all its emotion to Him who is our powerful healer. At a talk in Vancouver, John Swinton, a Scottish theologian, spoke about how the third book of Psalms (Psalms 73-89) is lament. "God has given us a language to describe sadness, joy." He shares that Scripture "encompasses all of our emotions." Lamenting is about expressing our grief and disappointment. The words written in the Psalms guide us in a prayer of grief.

On summer nights I struggle with depression, "my eyes grow dim with sorrow" (Psalm 88:9). Psalm 88, among many others, speaks of sadness. Holding fast to God's unchanging love for me, I pray as best I can. I praise Him through listening to worship songs. By walking in nature. I notice the shape of the red-tinged clouds at sunset. The scent from jasmine blossoms. I make rhubarb sauce with orange zest.

For a meaningful connection with God, I imagine visiting a lonely, closed church to find Jesus present in a tabernacle and talk to him as a friend. That way He is no longer alone. I do not like the feeling of being alone. He is with me in my darkness. He reminds me that I matter. He delights in me. You matter. You are a delight. Jesus is close to you. The Lord's redemptive love wraps us in safety and heals our brokenness.

Read Psalm 88 and pray in your own unique way. Talk to God with how you are feeling and be grateful that he accepts your imperfect prayer.

4. Finding purpose out of darkness

Have you ever wondered why you are on this earth? What you were made for? Why you struggle in a certain way?

I have been reflecting on the turbulent years when I suffered seriously with mental illness. I wanted to find happiness. I wanted to find wellness. I wondered, what was the point of this anguish?

As I began the journey of finding help, and health, I also became a hope finder. My most profound experience of hope is living out my Catholic faith. I discovered the power of prayer, receiving the sacraments, reflecting on Scripture, and regularly confessing my sins. I began to believe that I am beloved. That I am *not* my illness, I *have* an illness. I am a precious daughter of God, and my worth comes from him.

After much therapy and opening-up to friends with my story, I found peace in owning my challenge and using it to guide others. Talking about mental health and resilience shatters the stigma that I hold about having an invisible illness. I realized, my story is not my own, and by releasing it, it becomes a story of victory. Christ died and rose from the dead to bring me new life. In my times of darkness, when I was despairing, Jesus was with me the whole time. He never abandoned me and never will. Maybe I was meant to come out of the pain and to share with people in the thick of it that there is hope. That life is worth living. That it gets better.

In the podcast *Cathy Heller Presents Don't Keep Your Day Job,* Heller says, "I believe that the opposite of depression is not happiness; it's purpose. I believe that every single person has something unique to contribute to the world."

I hold fast to the words of the prophet Jeremiah, "For I know the plans I have for you, says the Lord, plans for welfare and not for evil, to give a future and a hope" (Jeremiah 29:11).

Finding purpose out of darkness is God's pièce de résistance in our lives. Sharing my story is healing, as is revealing the hope that I hold—and that everyone can have hold of, too.

I waited at my desk for the film crew to arrive. I hadn't eaten much. My appetite left when I anticipated the hour I would share my story. The afternoon went by and only a couple coworkers remained in the office.

The crew set up the camera and lights in the chapel. As I strolled through the halls of the Archdiocese with the CEO, Daniel Whitehead, I shared my excitement at the opportunity to share my story of living with bipolar disorder.

Sitting in the chapel, I could feel the Lord's presence in me, and my nerves calmed. It took me years to get to this place of vulnerability. I answered Daniel's questions with serenity. It felt like the Holy Spirit flowed through me and into my speech.

I wasn't always ready to talk about my struggles with mental illness. I wanted to start a blog and keep it anonymous. Then I decided that anonymity would perpetuate stigma. When I finally published the blog *The Resilient Catholic*, I posted a photo of myself and used my name.

I still can get hung up on the label of bipolar disorder. I know that I am not my illness, I have an illness. If I read something negative on social media or in the news about bipolar disorder, it weighs on me.

I hoped that telling my story would help someone feel less alone and reach for help.

Everyone struggles with something. If you have a mental illness, you are going to be okay. Each new day is an opportunity to discover the unique call God has for my vital life. With wonder and awe, I seek his will for this beautiful and messy masterpiece. Sometimes, it's about offering up my suffering, knowing that this too has purpose.

Find out more about the Sanctuary Course for Catholics at https://sanctuarymentalhealth.org/catholics/ or at formed.org. For the Ecumenical Sanctuary Course https://sanctuarymentalhealth.org/sanctuary-course/.

The filming that I was involved in was for *The Sanctuary Course for Catholics*. This resource has testimonial videos focused on eight individuals' stories, mine included.

In the study you will read, process, and discuss topics on themes such as "understanding mental health and mental illness, challenging stigma, and the recovery journey."

The eight-part course for small groups is intended to "bring hope and healing to people and churches across Canada." It's a tool to help people of faith learn how to "sensitively create communities of care for those of us facing mental health challenges." You may know a family member, a friend, a colleague, or someone who struggles with mental illness. This is a great opportunity to discover more about self-care, companionship, and caregiving.

5. It takes a forest to lift a spirit

Intertwining branches of tall mossy trees reach out. My heart feels free to enjoy the day. I breathe in the scent of nature's cathedral. Oxygen refreshes my lungs and gives me a giddy feeling of lightness.

Hiking with friends, our pace is quick, our strides match as we climb around rocks and over roots. Moments of not talking. Bird calls. Wind swishing evergreen branches. The clomp of hiking boots on packed earth. This is our music. My body relaxes, becomes calm. Hiking grounds me and connects me to our Creator.

Respite and recovery liberate my mind and spirit. I needed this walk through a canopy of trees. Stopping for almond snacks, chocolate bark, and cool sips of water, I am energized to continue. Almost at the falls. Our conversation and laughter fill the air around us.

"Careful!" my friend points to stinging nettle at the path's edge. I study its light green leaves and step om it. Falling pine needles hit my hat. I delight ..sy stones, old man's beard, and crackly bark.

In Peter Wohlleben's book, *The Hidden Life of Trees*, he explains that a forest is a community. The trees "exchanges nutrients" to help "neighbours in times of need." "A tree is not a forest. On its own, a tree cannot establish a consistent local climate. It is at the mercy of wind and weather." Many trees together create a "protected environment." "Trees can live to be very old."

Just as I thrive in nature I can count on the support and encouragement of my community. Like the mother trees shading young saplings to not grow too fast, my mother nurtured my growth as a child. She was there when I needed help the most. In a moment of despair when I had lost all hope, she intervened and with her tireless care, I received the best aid. Medicine, therapy, prayer, and love. In times of recovery, walking in nature gives me the opportunity to wonder.

My family, friends, and colleagues are the community that aids my growth and well-being. I am grateful for their love and kindness. My world is colourful and bright with the phone calls, visits, gifts and affection from them.

Fungi dot the ground. Fiddleheads unfurl. The sound of water rushes over rocks. We are close. Up a steep incline. Quick short breaths. Reach for the last step to view Norvan Falls.

The two-hour hike was worth the view. Lush green trees surrounding the wild creek bed. Smooth rocks with cold glacier water tumbling over them. Sunlight streaming through the canopy of branches. Where would I be without the help of my family and friends? Isolated. Sad. Hopeless. Life would be more like a desert than a forest.

I breathe deeply and smile at my fellow hikers: friends, sisters. We made it. No matter what, we all need someone to help us in difficult times. Everyone needs a team to encourage, motivate, and speak truth into our hearts.

Jesus, the good shepherd knows how much we need peace. "He makes me lie down in green pastures. He leads me beside still waters. He restores my soul. (Psalm 23:2-3).

Hiking gives me the ability to rest in interior and exterior peace. To grow in friendship and love. To find joy in another's presence and to stay healthy physically and mentally.

Connecting to the Creator among the trees strengthens my drive for life. "Even though I walk through the valley of death, I fear no evil; for you are with me; your rod and your staff, they comfort me" (Psalm 23:4).

Give yourself the treat of walking in nature. Practice slow looking—taking in the scents and sounds around you.

6. Confession: a race to mercy

Dim lights. Knees to velvet kneeler. Quiet contrite conversation in a room as big as a broom closet. This is being relentless in the spiritual life.

Returning again and again to the redeeming sacrament of confession, no matter how many times I confess the same sins. A race to mercy.

I don't want to drag my feet. Though I still do. Instead, I give up the feeling of hopelessness by remembering Jesus' mercy. I walk right back into the open arms of my dearest friend Jesus Christ.

My goal is to confess often. To go back to the well. The Lord has living water. Refreshment for the mind and soul. And my thirst is mighty. Saints get up from sin over and over again. They open themselves up to grace.

I never tire of receiving joy from confessing my sins. I fall down, but Jesus remains at my side.

Once the priest has given me absolution, I drink the peace and joy of salvation. When I open the door of the confessional to pray my penance, a lightness expands in my heart.

Restoration. Inner healing. Peace in body, mind, and soul. "The steadfast love of the Lord never ceases, his mercies never come to an end; they are new every morning; great is your faithfulness" (Lamentations 3:22-23).

Recently, I met up with my childhood friend at a favourite Poke restaurant. We ordered take-out to eat at a rooftop garden in the heart of the city.

After we hugged and stood in line to order, Allixe looked at me and said, "Something is different about you, Lisa. You look good … confident."

Smiling, I mulled over possible reasons for this compliment. No new haircut. Or clothes. Must be something else.

"Well, I did come straight from confession."

A soul cleanse.

"I thought that is why you might have picked this location, since it's near the cathedral." She dug deeper. "How does it make you feel?"

"Fresh. Like I can begin again."

The conversation switched to her upcoming travel plans. We ordered our dishes. My heart was singing and doing back flips. I was so happy. Hope-filled that this time, healing from a particular sin happened. I know I had encountered Jesus. The peace after confession is warm sunshine on my face.

My parents modelled the blessing of frequent confession. As a young girl, I would visit the chapel on a Saturday morning with my parents and siblings. The promise of ice cream or time to play on the playground afterwards sweetened the deal. Sweeter than chocolate mint ice cream was the feeling of interior freedom.

The sacrament of confession has the capacity to shine light from inside our soul onto our face. It's not surprising that we become like little lamps. For the Lord is the light of the world. When we open our hearts to receive his grace, our cup overflows.

Don't let repetitive sins weigh you down. There is always confession. Never give up. "… For you know the testing of your faith produces steadfastness; and let steadfastness have its full effect, so that you may be perfect and complete, lacking in nothing." (James 1:3-4)

Be encouraged by Jesus' mercy and go to confession.

7. Healing comes in surprising ways

Sweet scents from white flowering bushes were my first encounter with her incredible garden.

I walked by Margaret's garden often in my quiet Vancouver neighbourhood. A tall chestnut tree stands guard and bark mulch covers the ground where plants look wild and less manicured.

Her smile invited conversation as she raked leaves. Curly grey hair framed her round face. As our friendship grew, she told me about her trip alone on a ship to Canada, and her long days working on the family farm in Germany.

We found shared interests in classical music, in the beauty of flowers, and the simple pleasure of fresh garden vegetables. Our fondness of magnolias held our unlikely friendship together, as did our shared ache for family, health, and happiness.

Arise Shine & Live

After a run along the seawall I passed by her house. My dear neighbour was sweeping the sidewalk. Arthritis and sore knees don't keep her from her garden. Strength still flows through her aging body.

Inviting me to sit on her front steps, we enjoyed the sunset and purple rhododendrons that were starting to bloom, squirrels scampering, and trees coated in gold.

Our laughter filled the air. My delight in her tender care of the plants connected us to the goodness of nature, new every season. From the steps before her red door, I looked up. A canopy of spring green leaves and a soft spray of chestnut flowers filled the sky.

Healing comes in surprising ways. The peaceful presence of a neighbour. Time to chat. Watching her pick beets from the dirt in her garden for my dinner. Listening to her story of overcoming challenges and learning about her rough life yet resilient soul.

Her endearing character shines through her garden and her smiling eyes. Carefree timelessness restores my soul. Being too busy all the time takes a toll on my mental health. I relish moments with Margaret that slow me down and fill my heart with love.

I've only known her a few years, but I feel at home when I walk by her garden and see her smile.

Knowing I belong to God my heavenly Father, I also feel secure. His love is like a patient gardener. He tends to the thorns and weeds found in times of depression, pruning and clipping.

When life is overwhelming, He finds a way to root me in hope so I flourish again. Never a day goes by without some work. My mental health withers without care. More and more I am learning to lean on God. To surrender. To trust Him in everything.

I still falter. It is unfinished work. I like to think that I am His beloved wildflower. Storms will come, winds and rain, and bugs. But He will not leave me in darkness. He loves me and will bring me to the light.

"The Lord created medicines from the earth" (Sirach 38:4) and beautiful flowers in Margaret's garden.

"And a sensible man will not despise them ... By them he heals and takes away pain; the pharmacist makes them a compound" (Sirach 38:4,7).

How marvelous that God gives us the means to be well. Skills of physicians, medicines, and loving relationships bring about healing. We can rely on the Lord, "for the sake of preserving life" (Sirach 38:14). Do not give up hope. Hope in the Lord. He is with you always.

Buy flowers to brighten your home. They could be freshly cut or in a pot. Whatever you prefer.

8. Whether your song is happy or sad, God is listening

"It's a gift to exist and with existence comes suffering. There is no escaping that," said Stephen Colbert in an interview with Anderson Cooper on grief. He went on to say, "There is no other timeline. This is it. The bravest thing you can do is accept the world as it is."

As a depressed teenager I lost sight of hope. I couldn't come up with any reasons to live. To stay here. I didn't understand how treasured I was. By God. By my family and friends. It's beautiful to discover that we were born into this world for a purpose. That life is good even when it comes with suffering. To experience happiness, you must also experience loss. A rich mix of emotions makes us human.

I am blessed with many graces that help me thrive here in Vancouver. Being surrounded by lush nature. Family close by. Fulfilling work. Diversity in dining. A welcoming church community. Friendly neighbours.

I am grateful that I can enjoy it all with my healthy body.

One cool evening, after not running for an entire month to avoid the summer heat, I laced up my runners. Breathing in and out quickly. My muscles stretched like a cat's after a nap. The view was as beautiful as ever. Passing cyclists smiled and nodded, affirming my effort. Stopping at a crosswalk, I thought about quitting to get dinner, but I knew that further along the seawall there was a better view of the water. I pushed on. In slow mode.

Once at the oceanside, I breathed in deeply. Music twirled in the air from the community piano. After the young woman finished a classical piece, I rushed to it. Beads of sweat fell along my hairline as I played. In these ordinary moments I realized life is all right. That we are unique and irreplaceable. We all have a song to sing. God doesn't leave us in the darkness. The light rushes in. Growth happens. We emerge stronger than before.

Having lived in days of darkness gives me the capacity to connect with people on a raw and profoundly human level. Empathy, a gift of understanding someone else's suffering, is something I have felt too. Everyone experiences grief, loss, or pain. When we can share a moment with another, we promise they are not alone.

A French-speaking man smiles and moves toward the piano saying, "Bravo."

"Do you want to play?" I ask.

He sits and sings, stroking the keys of the brightly painted outdoor piano. Each of us giving a free concert to an intimate crowd. Making a gift of ourselves, we are "not simply a 'being' but always a 'being for'" (Pacific Institute of Family Education).

"You clothed me with skin and flesh, and knit me together with bones and sinews. You have granted me life and steadfast love, and your care has preserved my spirit" (Job 10:11-12).

The longer I live, the more grateful I am for each breath. I will bless the Lord with my comings and goings, knowing how deeply He loves me. Knowing that He suffered too. That joy awaits us in the kingdom that He has opened to us.

Listen to your favourite song or album.

9. Jesus' resurrection fuels my joy

He is alive!

The cheerful feeling Easter brings is indescribable. My heart beats with newness. Sunshine warms my face as I walk home anticipating a meal with my sister. Flowers fill my neighbours' garden beds. Bright tulips. Bird songs. Later sunsets. Foil wrapped chocolates.

This joy is not dependent on these fleeting delights. "Behold, I am doing a new thing" (Isaiah 43:19). Jesus' resurrection is the greatest gift I will receive. Heavenly happiness. The excitement of knowing the Saviour has opened the gates of heaven and is preparing a room for me, for you. This knowledge fuels a deep abiding joy that no illness, obstacle, fear, or disaster can take away.

There are many high and low times with a mental illness. During the lows, I find ways to bring back joy. Taking extra care of my body and spirit is essential.

Delicious home-cooked meals, steaming cups of tea, and a good night's sleep all ease sorrow.

A chicken dinner with roast vegetables may not seem like a remedy for anything but hunger. I beg to differ. The aroma of garlic butter and crisping potatoes pushes out sadness. I smile as I breathe in the scent of the warm dinner. Eating it in company is always better. The intimacy of the table creates conversations of interest and confidence. Moist meat falls off the bone and vegetables are sprinkled with spice. It's a beautiful blessing to share a meal and nourish the body.

My spirit revives with the sacraments. Daily Mass. Recitation of the Rosary. Adoration. Frequent confession. Reception of the Holy Eucharist. Thin white wafer. Jesus' body and blood. Immeasurable spiritual results.

I often kneel in the chapel marveling at the cost of salvation. Jesus died and rose again. For me. For you. It takes a strong relationship to look at the crucifix and understand the depth of His love. The suffering that He endured astounds me.

When kneeling in adoration of the Lord's presence, I silence the worries and doubts and place my trust in Him. In Pope Francis' homily for the Easter Vigil, he said, "let us put the Living One at the centre of our lives. Let us ask for the grace not to be carried by the current, the sea of our problems; the grace not to run aground on the shoals of sin or crash on the reefs of discouragement and fear. Let us seek him in all things and above all things. With him, we will rise again." Freedom from sorrow comes when I trust in the Lord. My joy comes from my faith in God.

Lyrics from a song by Raffi remind me that we don't need a lot to be happy. "All I really need is a song in my heart, food in my belly, and love in my family."

Heavenly happiness is in reach at all times. When we are hungry, or lonely, or depressed, "the Lord is my strength and my shield; in whom my heart trusts" (Psalm 28:7).

The joy of Easter can be carried through the year. "We do not pretend that life is all beauty. We are aware of darkness and sin, of poverty and pain. But we know Jesus has conquered sin and passed through his own pain to the glory of the Resurrection. And we live in the light of his Paschal Mystery – the mystery of his Death and Resurrection. We are an Easter People and Alleluia is our song!" (Saint Pope John Paul II).

I will let this Alleluia song become my anthem for my life. It reminds me to give all my experiences to Jesus who can redeem them all. The ability to get up again and again from difficult circumstances is rising from pain.

Jesus gives us his light to be resilient. We can give Him our grief and trust in his undeniable love for us. And we can also cook a mouth-watering chicken dinner.

Cook and share a favourite meal with family members or friends.

10. We need the support of others

Welcomed. Seen. Heard. The support group meeting helped me to overcome the stigma around having a mental illness.

Four years ago, I walked into a neighbourhood church meeting room with mismatched couches and chairs and was welcomed by a friendly face. The facilitator offered me a hot cup of tea, and I instantly felt more at ease as I held the ceramic mug. A few more people trickled in. The meeting opened with prayer and introductions.

I was surprised by how everyone had a mental illness and yet they were working, living, and doing it all with perseverance. Mental illnesses are invisible. If the meeting attendees hadn't been courageous and vulnerable while sharing in the group, I would never have guessed they battled mental illness. People who experience anxiety, depression, and eating disorders are fighters. It was so comforting to meet other mental health warriors who have faith in God, who is with us through it all.

Once I received a brief text message from one of the members, saying he had fallen ill. "Can you talk?" I sent a message back to him with a couple of questions like those used by Kevin Briggs, who is known as the Guardian of the Golden Gate. Kevin was with the California Highway Patrol and prevented many suicides by talking and listening to the troubled souls.

I asked, "Are you okay tonight? What are your plans for tomorrow? I am free to chat tonight."

He responded, "I'll call in fifteen."

During that phone call I felt connected to someone who may not have had anyone else to call.

After 45 minutes of listening, I asked, "Can we pray to God for protection?"

"Yes, please," was his reply.

The next day, he emailed saying, "It's a miracle. I feel much better this morning! Thank you for listening to me."

Weeks later, it was my turn to call him for a listening ear. I needed someone to talk to. Someone who understands what it's like to have uncomfortable symptoms of illness return in times of stress.

I am inspired by Henry Fraser, author of *The Little Big Things: A Young Man's Belief that Every Day can be a Good Day*. When he was a teenager, he dove into the ocean and was paralyzed from the shoulders down. While recovering in the hospital, Henry saw a man with a similar spinal cord injury wheel himself out of the hospital in a wheelchair. He was determined to do the same. "Disabled people need to see themselves in others. We need to see others like us achieving, living and inspiring." Being present with members of the support group has been instrumental in pushing myself to carry on. Resilient people can't thrive all on their own. We need the support of others.

I will continue to brave the rain and walk to the group hoping to lift someone else up, as so many do for me. I try to view my illness as a grace. I don't like the crippling sadness or the fears that invade my thoughts at times. But the sadness passes, and when it does, everything is sweeter.

Hope pervades my heart when I am in the presence of another. "I said, 'I am falling'; but your constant love, O Lord, held me up. Whenever I am anxious and worried, you comfort me and make me glad" (Psalms 94:18-19).

Community brings peace and reminds me that I am not alone. Our inner lives are so important. Within our hearts, we can talk to our Saviour who is always with us. It's a blessing to be able to pray with a friend on a difficult night, sharing in their struggle. Stronger than any medicine is the company of a kind and caring friend. My life matters. Your life matters.

Call a friend you haven't spoken to in a while.

11. On being salty and bright

In summer, I love spending time at the beach in salty air with sandy feet. On the rocky beach at Lighthouse Park, I notice changes to the wooden dock. It looked new, with a fresh coat of paint. Yet the lighthouse remains the same. A simple construction of steel with a light at the top.

I remember someone who was a lighthouse for me on stormy days when I was confined in a psychiatric ward the first time with bipolar disorder. I was bored, fatigued, and longing to be well. With only TV, magazines, and meals to occupy my time, the hours dragged on. Flipping through *Today's Parent* and *Style* magazines did not entertain me for long. My family visited often, bringing hugs and a dose of much needed laughter.

When I was struggling, I treasured moments in nature more than I had before. Short, fifteen-minute walks made the hospital garden, with its stone path and rose bushes, a place of solace for me. The nurse's aide who accompanied us was open to talking with me about my ideas for life after the hospital. She was a bright shining light of hope.

I looked forward to our visits in the garden. Not only was it a chance to leave the hospital ward, but it was also an opportunity to trust in the Lord's healing mercy. The nurse's aide's smile filled the room as she invited anyone interested to "escape" for a while and breathe in fresh air. She had a peacefulness about her that calmed my nerves. Our conversation was always light but could deepen in an instant. After a couple of weeks, I wanted to be like her, study her profession, and share the same joy for life.

I still seek out gardens and wild open spaces to clear my mind and unwind. Every summer my family and I find time to relax by the ocean. Hearing waves crash, sea gulls call, and wind in the trees transports me to carefree happiness. The salty scent of seaweed and the peachy warm sunsets are worth the long drive. I love the carefree time with my family on these trips. If the weather permits, we gather around a campfire singing songs and roasting marshmallows.

In the Gospel of Matthew, Jesus speaks about being salt of the earth and light of the world. Without salt there is no flavour. Without light a town on a hill can be hidden. The kind nurse's aide had both. The memory of her name escapes me, but these words from Scripture soak in like summer sunshine and salty air.

Let us be salty and bright. Our presence to others—the nurse's aide to a patient—can bring faith to a forlorn soul. I will always remember her smile and readiness to listen in my time of turmoil.

An ocean swim will be a great reminder to stay salty, and when I gaze up at the stars from my campsite, they'll encourage me to be bright.

Read Matthew 5:13-14 and think about what encourages you to be salty and full of light.

12. Never give up on hope

It's not that I wanted to die. I wanted to escape the unbearable pain.

"Are you okay?" my mom asked me.

"No, I am not okay." I was seventeen years old, and I thought there was no point living anymore. I thought my family would be better off without me. Despair doesn't give you company. It leaves you alone, in your pain, with tears, and feeling hopelessness.

Deeply sad, I uttered the words, "Help me!" and somehow God triumphed. My mom found me scared, helpless, and crying on the bathroom floor. I couldn't lift myself up. She held me tenderly and helped me dress in my fuzzy pajamas.

My intense emotion began to thaw as her gentle hands led me to the living room and helped me to sit at the piano. As she made phone calls— "Lisa will not be going on the overnight Grade 12 retreat tomorrow" —I plunked the piano keys, playing my favourite song, "Only Hope." After a few songs, I crumpled on

Arise Shine & Live

the ground crying louder, shaking, and shouting, "Get the devil off me!" My mom calmly said, "Dad and I are going to take you to the hospital." Her hands rested on my back, moving in slow soothing circles as she prayed audibly.

No one knew what was wrong. No one knew that I was suffering an episode of psychosis, a break from reality. The hallucinations, negative thoughts, and despair were all a part of it. My younger sister helped me down the stairs, as I, shaking with fear, leaned all my weight on her.

That hospital stay was the beginning of my journey from mental illness to health. Somehow, hope snuck into my home and my heart. Attentiveness from my mother and affection from my sister bolstered me. I will never forget the kindness of my family during that time. They are heroes and healers. I love them immensely.

In November, we pray for the souls of the departed. Most of us know someone who took his or her own life or know someone who has been affected by the suicide of a loved one. In my prayers, I remember my dear cousin who took her life a couple of years ago.

The Catechism tells us: "Grave psychological disturbances, anguish, or grave fear of hardship, suffering, or torture can diminish the responsibility of the one committing suicide. We should not despair of the eternal salvation of persons who have taken their own lives. By ways known to him alone, God can provide opportunity for salutary repentance. The Church prays for persons who have taken their own lives" (Part 3, article 5 2282-2283).

As I paced those hospital halls at age 17, I gripped my rosary in my hand and held on to hope even when I couldn't recite the prayers. In the wisdom of St. John Paul II, "I plead with you—never, ever give up on hope, never doubt, never tire, and never become discouraged. Be not afraid."

Let us pray with St. Faustina, "Jesus, I trust in you!"

Father Chris Alar shares that there is "hope for those who've committed suicide" in the pamphlet *Divine Mercy After Suicide*. He encourages us to pray the Divine Mercy chaplet for the deceased, because God is outside of time. "This is the power of prayer, even for those who have taken their own lives or who have died years ago."

Pray the Divine Mercy Chaplet or a prayer you know well for those you love.

13. Baby Jesus brings joy to a hurting soul

After a month in a psychiatric ward, I looked forward to going home to comfortable surroundings. Instead, after my discharge, I moved into a house with four other adults who also had chronic disabilities. My support team believed this was the best step forward. I faced this new adventure with trepidation, as I waited for a breakthrough in my mental health.

We grocery shopped, cooked for each other, took turns with chores, and volunteered in the community. Our schedules were given to us with little consultation, but the weekends were ours to plan.

I took a three-hour bus ride to visit my family each Saturday and returned Sunday night. I made this weekly trip for seven months. The commute was frustrating but seeing my parents, brothers and sisters was worth it.

My time in the group home was bittersweet. I shared a room with someone who woke up before me and would make light and noise fill the room. Having the tv room to myself most evenings was great. Walking to the library, coffee shops and gym helped to fill my time as well. Christmas approached, and I spent quiet evenings in the kitchen making crafts. As I painted, knitted and decorated, I reflected on my blessings. Advent is a time of waiting. Waiting for the perfect gift. A king. A little baby. How adorable. How humble.

Being away from home, I focused on the little things I could change in my life. Being happy that Mary said "Yes." That Jesus became flesh. I spent afternoons working out in the gym, swimming, reading in the library, and visiting the elderly at the seniors home where I volunteered.

I participated in everything they suggested: walks, baking cookies, singing carols. The challenge was—and still is—not to become too busy with shopping, parties, and preparations. Otherwise, I lose sight of the true light and meaning of Christmas. My mental health suffers if I become too busy doing, instead of being.

I look back now with gratitude at that time of growth and that place to heal my mind, when I was 18 years old. My health and well-being have transformed since those times of deep depression and anxiety. I still struggle. My illness is lifelong and has ups and downs, but a light shines even on my darkest days: the gift of Jesus' love in my life. Little baby Jesus brings joy even to a hurting soul. I wait in excited anticipation for the peace He brings wrapped in swaddling clothes.

The Saviour of the world didn't arrive in comfort. In the darkest time of year, in the chaos of a messy stable, Jesus came to us in a simple way. He was dependent on Mary and Joseph for everything.

If I were to put myself in the nativity story, instead of rushing around, I would hold Jesus in my arms. Mary would be resting beside me and Joseph telling a bedtime story, like my Dad did for me. I would sing Jesus a happy song, accompanied on my ukulele, praising His majesty. I would bring Him some homemade speculaas cookies that taste like gingerbread. If I sat by His creche, my mind would calm, and I would find sanity in adoration of Him.

Christmas is a time of joy, but sometimes we must choose to experience it. It fills me with peace that I am not alone. I am happiest when I place Him at the centre of my life. The first Christmas after my diagnosis of bipolar disorder was full of love. My family came together and built a gingerbread house decorated with candy. We sang carols for our friends and neighbours. Instead of isolating myself and tucking away from it all, I was the gift.

I am blessed with a nurturing family that helped me embrace the joy of Christmas. We can carry the anticipation of Advent throughout the year. Expecting Jesus to show up when we need Him. Ask Him for anything you need, adore Him, and spend time in His presence.

Spend some time in an Adoration Chapel and slow down in Jesus' sweet presence.

14. Quebec churches cured my cold and loneliness

Quebec City. Snow piled high. Icy footsteps on the sidewalk. Adventuring, alone. Black winter boots, a toque, and a splash of homesickness.

It was the winter of 2008. Four years had passed since I was in the group home. Christmas over, I travelled to Quebec to live there for a year. The program Une Année pour Dieu (A Year for God) was a time of discernment. I sought to know if God was calling me to a religious vocation. I also volunteered for the Diocese of Quebec, joining a group of eight young adults preparing for the 49th Eucharistic Congress and discovering our vocations.

Had I been able to speak French fluently, I would have felt more at home. I missed a flight and hardly slept while hugging my luggage in the airport. I had just visited my family for Christmas, and after arriving at the convent of the Sisters of The Good Shepherd, I went straight to bed. I was extremely

Arise Shine & Live

fatigued by the long trip and slept almost a whole day. The Sisters thought I had died because I slept so long. But the following evening when they heard the fridge door open in the middle of the night, they were relieved that I had awoken.

Early mornings. A new language. Living in a convent and working at the Diocese of Quebec was so different from my regular routine back home. I prayed with the sisters in the morning and in the evening. I ate dinner and washed the dishes with them. I struggled to adjust to this new reality because of the language barrier and change in routine.

We were paired up to live in a convent or a monastery to learn more about the religious community we stayed with as part of the program. My French conversational skills needed improvement. I stayed with a new religious community, Famille Marie-Jeunesse in Sherbrooke for a few months before joining the rest of the team at the Diocese of Quebec. I had a private tutor and immersion to help me learn the language more quickly. I found an Anglophone friend who would chat with me in English at times. I think this slowed my lessons.

The side effects of my medication that helped balance my moods were uncomfortable, especially the cystic acne. It was difficult to get the help I needed using my limited French. The cold, long winters of eastern Canada surprised me. I ripped a pair of frozen jeans when I arrived at the diocese. I shovelled the snow away from the wrong basement bedroom window. I became frustrated and homesick and wanted to take the next plane home. The snow kept falling.

Looking for a cure for homesickness, I began making more phone calls to my family. My sister delighted me by sending my sheet music to play the piano in the convent. Joining a church choir with my friend and roommate Isabelle brought unexpected joy. Dinners, prayers, and Mass at the community of Famille Marie-Jeunesse gave me a sense of belonging.

Another antidote for homesickness was to go for walks with friends. We went sightseeing and strolled around the Plaines d'Abraham. The snow covered fields were beautiful. The twinkling lights in the streets filled with snow looked like a picture from a snow globe.

I watched with wonder as my friend Isabelle became close to the community of nuns at the Dominicaines Missionnaires Adoratrices. We visited their convent at Easter for a retreat. It was a lot of fun. While on my way to the chapel, I was deciding, *Chocolat ou Jesus? Les deux! Both!* I picked up a chocolate from the novitiate room and then went to adoration with the chocolate melting in my mouth.

When we were on dish duty, we stifled our giggles. We found it very difficult to follow the rule to work in silence. We walked around the grounds and took turns seeking counsel with the directrice. Isabelle joined this community as a sister after the program finished.

The program provided immersion in a religious community, opportunities to pray and learn from each other's experiences, and to work at the Diocese.

We participated in a pilgrimage to Montreal that stopped at St. Joseph's Oratory. It is an amazing church with a rich history that includes Saint Brother André Bessette. Many miracles happened there because of his holiness and intercession. I want to be holy like him. There is a wall of crutches that people have left there after being healed. I saw his humble dwelling next door to the Oratory, and I watched as pilgrims climbed up the long flight of stairs to the church on their knees.

Since Quebec City was hosting the International Eucharistic Congress, most churches were open in the evenings for silent adoration. Bundled up in my winter gear, I trekked through snowy streets to beautiful old churches. Ice covered the tree branches and hung with icicles. Walking uncluttered my mind, and an hour of adoration cheered my heart. All of the activities and experiences in the program helped me to discern if I was called to religious life.

As my time in Quebec ended, I made a few realizations. First, I wasn't called to the consecrated life. I was receiving the sacraments every day—Mass, times of prayer, adoration, praying the rosary in community, and it still felt like someone was missing. One night, while praying in my bedroom in Sherbrooke, I looked at a picture of Mary and had a sense that someone was missing in my heart and it wasn't Jesus. I knew then that I was meant for the vocation of marriage. I decided to finish the year off because the big event—the 49th Eucharistic Congress was happening in the summer, and I wanted to be a part of it.

Second, I can be fearless, even while living with bipolar disorder. Moving across the country to discern God's call, all while learning to speak a new language, took courage. This self-knowledge has helped me to challenge myself in different areas of my life. When I returned home, I continued to speak French, not wanting to lose the language. Occasionally, I even dream in French.

Arise Shine & Live

Homesickness reveals our love of family and desire for connection. Staying focused on my goals and keeping in touch with family and friends helped get me through the year. Openness to where God is calling me in my vocation helps me to hear His voice. For now, I am living out my vocation as a single professional, daughter, sister, godmother, and friend. The Lord knows the timing of when I will be called to marriage. He created me out of love and for love.

I sought a community when I returned home that could further my spiritual formation and was introduced to Opus Dei, The Work of God. It is a Roman Catholic lay and clerical organization whose members seek holiness by applying Christian ideals and values in every occupation in society. I attend recollections, meditations, and retreats to grow and be formed in the faith.

"Man was created for greatness—for God himself; he was created to be filled by God. But his heart is too small for the greatness to which it is destined. It must be stretched" (Pope Benedict XVI).

Find a quiet time for prayer. Talk to God like you would a friend and listen in silence.

15. Delicious dessert—a divine gift

I polished off the salty beef and stared warily at the neon pink pudding on my hospital tray.

Luckily the lady sitting beside me—I'll call her Pam—loves the colour pink. Pam has dementia and doesn't talk a lot. I turned to her. "Pam, do you want my pink pudding?"

"Yes!"

She ate it with gusto. I looked around the long table in the psychiatric ward to see if anyone else's stomach had turned at the sight of the unnaturally coloured dessert. Everyone stared at their food disenchanted, but I don't think the food was the real problem.

Instead of pudding, I enjoyed the apple juice and tea. The meals were sub-par and only staved off the raging appetite, one of the side effects of the anti-psychotic medicine. This was my first time in an adult mental hospital, and I was still a teenager. I didn't know how long I would be there, but I could at least rely on Pam to eat my questionable desserts.

Food has such meaning and memory for me. One of my favourite desserts, besides ice cream, chocolate and pie ... okay, the list could go on ... is mango pudding. It's funny that the pink pudding was so disgusting to me, while the sunshine yellow of mango pudding brings me joy. I love eating it, making it, and sharing it.

At a baptism for my friend's daughter, I enjoyed the feast after the beautiful sacrament. I had just finished eating a few cubes of mango pudding and thought, *If only I could have more mango pudding!*

Then I received a text message from another friend. "Are you home? I have something to bring to you." I let her know when I would be home. I could have easily walked back to the dessert table, but continued my conversation with friends at my table instead.

An hour later, I opened my door, and to my surprise my friend was standing there holding a large container of ... mango pudding. The Lord hears all our thoughts, wishes, and prayers. If he can answer such a small, insignificant desire of mine, how much more will he grant the bigger desires of my heart?

Giggling, I welcomed my friend in for a cup of tea. After chatting with her, I shared my story and asked for her recipe. It was a family recipe that she kindly shared with me. Making mango pudding and sharing it at parties or with friends and family gives me so much happiness.

From an aversion to neon pink pudding in the hospital to a fondness for creamy mango pudding, I marvel at how both these desserts acted like messengers. God has better and more delicious plans for me than I have for myself. With God there is abundance. With God there is communion.

My hunger for more moves me to reach outside of myself. If I bake banana bread, I give some away. Lively family dinners are a regular affair. Eating lunch with colleagues refreshes my spirit for the rest of the day. Trust that God will give good gifts.

Here's to dessert and to the divine!

Make a dessert and share it or write in your journal about a favorite dessert and why it is important to you.

16. Stand by me, Lord

Who will heal me?

I walked to Mass in the cold air, feeling heavy with sadness.

I heard the birds singing and took out my earbuds. *This is nature's music*, I thought to myself, *and better than anything I have on my playlist.*

I snapped a photo of the purple and yellow crocuses grown by a café. My heart yearns and aches for spring—in both my environment and my interior life.

I treasure the season of Lent leading to Easter: a time for spiritual growth, self-sacrifice, and communion with Jesus.

I struggle daily to not fill the space in my heart meant for God with other things. Retail therapy and indulging in delicious food are among the most enticing distractions.

I have been reading a lot lately to lift my spirits, especially the Bible. I want to know the Lord more, so that I may know His love for me. The book of Sirach is a new discovery for me, full of rich wisdom. The Mass readings from Sirach are a balm to my heart. "Await God's patience, cling to Him and do not depart. Trust in God and he will help you; hope in Him and He will make your ways straight" (Sirach 2:3,6).

The questions that follow cause me to ponder. "Or who ever persevered in His commandments and was forsaken? Who ever trusted in the Lord and was put to shame?" (Sirach 2:10).

Each Lent, I meditate on the Way of the Cross, a set of readings from the gospels on Jesus' crucifixion and death. Jesus felt real pain and knows what it's like to lament. Our own illness, rejection, and despair can unite us to Him. He knows our pain. His death is not the end. Our hope is in the resurrection. His love redeems us.

I arrived a few minutes before Mass and settled into a pew, gazing at the tabernacle and the crucifix. Wanting the hope, healing, forgiveness, and mercy that the cross, Good Friday, the cold, empty tomb and the unfailing warmth of the Resurrection bring.

After Mass, I enjoyed a comforting latte with my friend Stephanie, tucked into a sunny café corner. Inspired by our conversation, I played her newest ukulele as she drove me home. Later, I listened to one of my favourite songs, *Stand by Me*, which I often play on my own ukulele.

The lyrics are few, but the message is clear. No matter what happens, "If the mountains should crumble to the sea, I won't cry ... no I won't shed a tear. Just as long as you stand by me." (Ben E. King, Stand by Me, 1961).

We all want love. We are love. Lent reminds us that Jesus is the greatest lover and friend. Jesus wants us to stand by Him. He wanted the presence of his disciples as He prayed in the Garden of Gethsemane. Dying and rising, He gave us everything, to the last drop.

This Lent I will stand by the Lord, relying on his strength when I am sad. I will take delight in his passion for me. I will sing and play *Stand by Me* on my little ukulele.

I am not the only one who aches for happiness. Jesus heals. As Sirach tells us, "A faithful friend is an elixir of life; and those who fear the Lord directs his friendship aright" (Sirach 6:16).

Find a song that lifts your spirits and sing along to it.

17. God wants us to be happy

"To fly higher we need tension," said Stephanie over dinner.

I had to agree with her. Flying a stunt kite one Sunday taught me this lesson.

Fall is a good time to curl up with a hot drink and a good book. But instead, my three brothers, future brother-in-law, and I took a stunt kite to the park one weekend.

This kite was hand-sewn by my older brother, Adrian. He salvaged a tent to create a functional stunt kite fitted with two types of poles. We were all excited to try it out one blustery day, perfect for flying.

Standing in the middle of a soccer field, we unwound the strings and assembled the poles. I watched with wonder as the guys took turns launching the kite in the air. They controlled it by slight movements with their hands. Elbows tucked in, moving only their wrists with small, focused actions.

In the first trial launches, little adjustments were necessary. Zap straps kept breaking, as the wind was strong and the poles were heavy. They switched the poles to bamboo, which made a huge difference.

We were all so engaged in flying the kite and helping each other to have the best flight. My worries and niggling stress from the week disappeared.

When they had each had a turn, they shouted, "Give it a try, Lisa!"

I hesitated. "I won't be good at it."

But my youngest brother laughed. He came over to show me how to fly the large kite. He reviewed the movements needed for launching and direction. I listened. Nothing like a little dose of sibling competition to boost me up.

With a great gust of wind, I tilted my hands back, pointed my thumbs toward me and it took off. The kite climbed high. All the guys were clapping and encouraging me. Flying the kite was exhilarating.

The kite pulled and strained against my hands. My youngest brother yelled, "Hold it tight! Pull back!" I did what he said. The kite went higher, soaring like the seagull that flew by. I dipped it side to side. I laughed as it fluttered. All my brothers cheered. They couldn't believe how long it was staying up in the air, especially on my first try. I felt the strings go taut, reminding me of the tension needed to hold with a partner in swing dancing.

Trees bordered the field. White clouds dotted the sky. My hair was blowing in the wind. I felt connected to the earth and its marvels. The power of the wind. The softness of the grass beneath my feet and the tall waving trees tinged with yellow, red, and orange.

I felt free next to my brothers while sunlight blanketed us as we looked up at the sky. Flying a kite is happiness. Making it do stunts is an extra dose of joy. God means for us to be happy in this life.

St. John XXIII said, "Only for today, I will be happy in the certainty that I was created to be happy, not only in the other world but also in this one."

In this life there will be hardship and happiness. The steadiness of God, His concern for us to live an abundant life, bring me to a place of peace. Flying a kite, I experienced authentic joy for life.

Find a quote that inspires you and put it in a place to remember.

18. Seasons of blues, seasons of beauty

Snowflakes—rare in Vancouver—fell on the morning of my birthday and reminded me of the story around my birth.

On that late November day, when my parents were ready to take me home from Grace Hospital, there was an unexpected snowstorm. As they drove through a blizzard to be welcomed home by my two brothers and grandma, they prayed. My Dad nicknamed me "Snowflake."

Winters are known for coldness, darkness, stark landscapes, bare trees, frost and snow. As humans, we go through seasons, like the passing year. With or without a mental illness, we face change. Even in the winter season of life, we are beautiful. Beauty comes from within, a quiet strength that shines through our hearts. "I praise you, for I am wondrously made; wonderful are your works! You know me right well;

my frame was not hidden from you" (Psalms 139:14-15).

I have noticed seasons of beauty in nature at Queen Elizabeth Park, a short walk from both my home and workplace. I wander over there on lunch breaks or visit on weekends. In warmer weather, I enjoy picnicking under the trees or playing ukulele on a blanket with my friend. Cherry blossom season is much appreciated, as are the tulips and the summer roses. But there is an austere beauty found in winter too, when the park is empty. Varied hues of green, red, orange, and brown array the earth like hot chocolate spices, warming the eyes. Small unnoticeable buds push through the soil. Buds hang from trees in anticipation for spring. The dormant trees stand inactive, but they survive the bitter cold. Birds that haven't migrated sing in the chill. Squawking ducks swim slowly in the pond.

I have to be patient with myself and others during the season of blues. When sadness comes, it takes effort to look for the good. It can feel lonely and cold. On overwhelming days, I remind myself that there can be a clear view of a sky thick with stars, a little glimmer of hope and beauty in humanity.

God created us unique, even more spectacular than each delicate and unrepeatable snowflake.

"Beauty will save the world," says Dostoevsky, and I agree. How beautiful it is that our God came as an infant to save us. The song of angels brought a message of hope to the shepherds who were the first adorers of the child Jesus.

We too can visit the Lord and reverently adore him in the tabernacle. He is there, hidden from our eyes, a beauty divine. The gift of love that Jesus is strengthens me in every season.

In difficult, sad, and worrisome times, be patient. Look for the stars, shining in the midnight blue. Keep watch for a sign of hope, like shoots in the soil. There are better things ahead. The miracle of life unfolds moment by moment. I sure don't want to miss it!

God can melt the grief, sorrow, and illness that grip us and replace them with hope, love, and joy. When we thank him for our life, we invite him to pour his love into our hearts. The beautiful Lord will console us. He silently endures depression with us. He only has to say the word and we will be healed.

Take a walk in a park and enjoy the beauty of nature.

19. Who are your Jedi?

My big family can agree on few things. The Star Wars Saga is one of those things.

The movies have been a family favourite since I was a little girl. We gathered in the living room, pulling chairs tightly around the small square TV. We competed for the best seats and shared bowls of homemade buttered popcorn. My parents delighted in sharing both their faith in God and their interest in adventure stories, like the movies that George Lucas created.

Each Christmas we went to the theatre to watch the latest Star Wars film. We took up eight seats, almost a whole row, trying not to disturb anyone as we passed bags of licorice nibs, chocolates, and salty popcorn back and forth.

One October, when I was thinking of what to dress up for Halloween, my eldest brother said, "Just throw your hair over your face and you can be Chewbacca." We both laughed and I rolled my eyes. "I would rather be Princess Leia!"

My family has struggled through many difficult times. We have endured illnesses, deaths of loved ones, and many more trials. The support I receive to help flourish with good mental health comes from their big hearts and triumphant spirits. I could never fully thrive without the love and care of each of my brothers, sisters, and my parents.

In *The Rise of Skywalker*, Poe tells his friends that the First Order (the enemies) wants you to think that you are alone. "We are not alone," he says.

Finn tells Rey before she embarks on a dangerous journey, "We go together. We're all in this ... till the end."

During Rey's Jedi training, Princess Leia reminds her to "be patient" and to listen to the voices of the Jedi.

When I am depressed or experiencing hypomania, which come with bipolar disorder, I am comforted by my loved ones who are my companions on my journey.

The saints are also friends I turn to in prayer for help. God is more present to me than I am to myself. He knows how many strands of hair are on my head. I don't. We are worthy of His love for us. We are worthy of life. Knowing that I am a daughter of God strengthens me to carry on. I can struggle longer and hold on to the hope of healing. In times of distress, I turn to my family and friends, the saints and to my Lord. His love is in me.

One of my favourite scenes from the movie *The Rise of Skywalker* is when the evil Emperor Palpatine says to Rey, "You are nothing. A scavenger girl is no match for the power in me. I am all the Sith."

Rey shouts back, "And I am all the Jedi." Then she defeats Emperor Palpatine with Luke and Leia's light sabers.

I do not need to fear or give up when it seems hopeless. I can always turn to Jesus. I have the Holy Spirit, and the love of the Father and the Son. And Mother Mary and the communion of saints. The Lord has my back. "I have told you these things, so that in me you may have peace. In this world you will have trouble. But take heart. I have overcome the world" (John 16:33).

The Star Wars Saga offers lessons in choosing love over power. It shows the glory of standing up for what is good and that we don't have to be afraid in the face of adversity.

Our Lord is great and glorious, and He has won the battle. We can choose His side in fighting for our friends, sons, daughters, husbands, wives, and homes.

When we know who we are, we can courageously live because we lack nothing in the love of God.

Recall one of your favourite memories and journal in gratitude about it.

20. Collect your blessings

Wind whipped my face as I pulled my tuque tightly over my ears. I walked along Kits Beach with my sister one blustery day.

The stormy waves crashed against the sand, and my mood ebbed and flowed like the tide. Sometimes I feel fine and then, in an instant, I feel extremely low. January and February are often the bluest times of the year for me.

Last year, I took an online course from Yale University called *Psychology and the Good Life*. Not surprisingly, sleeping for eight hours, meditating, doing something kind for others, and listing five gratitudes daily were scientifically proven to improve wellbeing. Making these practices a part of my daily routine takes effort. Happiness takes work.

I collect things I am grateful for, like beachcombing for pretty rocks. As soon as I started noticing all the wonderful things in my life, a warmth enveloped me. God's love is ever-present. He looks after the details.

Arise Shine & Live

The most precious blessings are the people He has woven into my days. I am rich in friendships, and I hope to share the wealth. I like to make new connections for people by introducing them to friends of mine. I enjoy each moment as it comes. I am grateful for many things.

When I went walking with my sister in the rain, I felt alive.

While playing games with my godson as we visited on a video call, I felt silly.

When dining with my youngest brother, Thomas at my favourite restaurant, I delighted in his conversation and in fine wine.

While playing ukulele with my Mom on a Sunday afternoon, I felt joyful.

When listening to live music with friends and dancing on a Friday night I felt exhilarated.

While going to Mass with my friend and her young daughter, I felt at home.

These are some things I am grateful for. For you it could be a clean house, a good cup of coffee, or the Super Bowl.

Rushing into the pew at the back of the crowded church, I smiled at my companions. My friend and her little girl were waiting for me. I slipped in as the entrance song ended.

During the Prayers of the Faithful, my friend's daughter reached out her little arms and asked me, "Which one do you want?"

Stickers of many colours and shapes were on display between her fingers. I pointed at a bright yellow sun. She peeled it off for me, and I stuck it on my hand. The sunshine sticker was a token of love.

It reminded me to look up as the host was being consecrated. Jesus, the true light offering Himself to me again. As well as His love and solace during a cold and dark month. I smiled at my friend and her beautiful daughter. I felt connected, a part of the family.

Growing in resilience builds confidence to carry on in adversity. It is possible to fight the blues with companionship, prayers, acting with kindness, and praising the Lord for the good things in your life.

The courage it takes for people to actively choose life is commendable. Struggles can weigh heavy on the mind, body, and soul. It is healthy to seek help and to brave change.

I have hope because I trust in the Lord's provision for me. I know He wants me to be free of pain and suffering. He can show me a way through depression, anxiety, and fear.

Bipolar disorder has been a tool to teach me to lean more on Christ's strength than on my own. He can calm the storm. "And he awoke and rebuked the wind, and said to the sea, 'Peace! Be still!' And the wind ceased and there was a great calm" (Mark 4:39).

I need to not be afraid. The Lord brings peace, and I will get up again and again. Gratitude and kindness are strategies that have made me happier. Collecting your blessings actually works.

You could make a list or simply recall your blessings.

21. Home is where God is

"If anyone loves me, he will keep my word and my Father will love him, and we will come to him and make our home with him" (John 14:23).

How can a place you've never been to feel like home? One cold February, Eliza and I travelled to Phoenix, Arizona, for a retreat.

Neither of us expected to feel like we had come home.

Lifting our heavy backpacks out of the cab from the airport, we laughed and smiled, admiring the variety of cacti growing in the neighbourhood. A colleague of ours, from the Archdiocese of Vancouver, set us up with a place to stay with one of her relatives.

The sun was shining, and we no longer needed our coats and scarves. When we left Vancouver at 4 a.m., the temperature was below zero. Here, doves cooed from surrounding trees. Palm trees dotted the yards and swayed in the distance.

We stood at the front door, where a large statue of Mother Mary greeted us. I knocked and the door opened immediately. A beautiful blonde woman smiled and opened her arms.

"You must be Maggie!" I said.

As soon as I passed the threshold, her arms wrapped me in a big hug.

Her home beautifully combined order and cheerfulness. The patio had a dining set to entertain guests. Her kitchen had a large island with a large bouquet of flowers in the middle. There was a bar beside the fireplace and a cozy wrap-around couch.

"Can I get you something to drink? We have beer, pop, and seltzer water. Feel free to help yourself to anything. Make this place yours."

We settled our things into her teenage daughter's bedroom and lounged on their large grey couch. Excitedly, we told Maggie about the retreat that would start the next day. Before she left to take her son to his older brothers' baseball games, she promised to take us out for margaritas and Mexican food when she and her husband returned.

I'd come to Phoenix worn-out in heart, mind, and body. My heart was heavy, my mind exhausted, and my lower back ached. It was no coincidence that

Arise Shine & Live

the theme of the retreat was Restore. Eliza and I both decided to come to the Phoenix because of the retreat's theme. It was organized by Blessed Is She, a ministry for women with a mission for community and prayer.

When Maggie came back with her son from the baseball games, her younger sister Stella popped by with her 2-week-old baby. Seeing the precious baby cradled in my travelling companion's arms made my heart swell. Maggie's close-knit family all live on the same block and visit each other frequently.

It rained hard on Saturday morning but that didn't rob us of our joy for the day. Stella's brother-in-law waited outside to drive us to St. Andrew the Apostle Parish for the retreat. He is an Uber driver, and our colleague's mother paid for our trip. Gratitude at this family's generosity overwhelmed us.

My heart needed healing. Negative thoughts had been spinning me into low moods. *I am not good enough. I am unlovable. I am alone.*

During times of worship and adoration, I heard words like a whisper fill me: "I will never leave you alone. I wanted you in your mother's womb. No pain, no loss is wasted. Do not be afraid. You are my delight. Find peace in me. I love you, my beloved daughter. There will be days of rain, but I am always shining brighter than the sun. I will provide for you."

The home we stayed in for those three nights was a refuge. The love Maggie showed for her family, her community, and her vocation of motherhood confirmed for me the boundless love of God.

A home restores. We desire to belong and to be missed when we go away.

In her book *100 Days to Brave*, Annie F. Downs says, "Do whatever it takes to expand your map. Because if you go where you've never gone before, you will see God like you've never seen him before."

God makes a home in our hearts. Our ultimate destination and eternal home is heaven. We long to return to the heart of the Father. And now, I also long to return to Arizona.

Journal about a place where you feel at home.

22. Resilience and resurrection in a pandemic

I have never felt such a strong hunger for the sacraments as in the days leading up to Easter 2022.

It is a strange time that we are living in right now. A global pandemic is striking fear and panic in me, and maybe in you too. Worries are overwhelming. What will happen to my family, job, finances, and way of life? I worry about the way our lives will look like in the coming months and years. With all this change unfolding rapidly, we can count on the resurrection of the Lord. He gives us everything we need.

In the "darkness of the tomb the Lord rose triumphant. Let's not lose confidence. Let's never give up. Because Jesus is alive. He is with us in every situation of our lives" (Miller).

Even more now, I turn to the Lord in prayer throughout the day. I share with him my fears and questions about what is going on. I wonder when

He will come and calm this storm. He gives me the strength to face difficult days.

The meaning of life is more than having enough toilet paper. Yes, I stocked up on food and planned healthy meals in the event I were to get sick. I was grateful to my landlords for leaving a few rolls of bathroom tissue at my door. Each day of self-isolation, as my emotions rose and fell, I let myself feel the feelings. I didn't shut off all the anxiety, because a little anxiety is good to protect myself from danger.

As I live through this ongoing pandemic, I am exercising the virtues of faith and resilience. I carve out more time for prayer with online Mass, Rosary podcasts, and spiritual reading. I embrace the peace these actions bring.

Now, a couple years into the pandemic, Mass is back to being in person. I like participating in the Mass much better in the church than online. The Mass uses all the senses to pray. We stand and kneel in adoration. We hear the word of God proclaimed. We can see the priest consecrate the bread and wine. We can smell the incense. We taste the bread when we receive communion. We touch our knees to the kneeler to venerate Christ.

I also listen to the needs of my mind and body. When I need a snack, I find a few carrots or a bowl of mango yogurt to eat. When I need to move, I go for a walk or dance to my favourite upbeat songs. I try to accept that there is an outbreak and find peace in the moment by taking action.

On my first day working from home, I woke up to my sister making oatmeal. I added fresh bananas and ate it with my coffee as the morning light filtered into the living room. After breakfast, we lit candles scented with frankincense and myrrh for daily Mass. We participated in the Mass in Bishop Barron's chapel on YouTube. We blessed each other with holy water and prayed in silence.

Sitting at my desk to work remotely on the projects from my office, I felt grateful. It's good to have meaningful work, to have purpose. "Without purpose," says Eric Greitens in his book *Resilience*, "we can survive – but we cannot flourish."

Talking to family and friends on the phone and connecting virtually with friends and communities takes the edge off my anxiety. Gifts are hidden in this darkness. I have joined a live stream Rosary, sung along with Josh Groban in his live performance on Facebook, watched operas streaming free on MetOpera.org, and laughed at penguins roaming the aquarium after hours on YouTube. We live in an age of amazing technology. As my friend said, "It's the world wide web of God's beauty."

The joy of Jesus' resurrection is contagious. Because of His generous love, I look for ways to show up and give to others. Eric Greitens explains, "We become what we do if we do it often enough. We act with courage, and we become courageous. We act with compassion, and we become compassionate. If we make resilient choices, we become resilient." When we believe in God, we receive a new hope-filled perspective.

While reading Scripture in the soft bedroom light before bed, I find Jesus' words comforting: "Do not be anxious about your life, what you eat or what you will drink, nor about your body, what you will put on ... But seek first the kingdom of God and his righteousness, and all these things will be added to you" (Matthew 6:25, 33).

This day is a gift. Looking back at it, I breathe deeply and ask, *Who will make these days brighter?* Closing my eyes, I feel deep gratitude for Jesus' love. The light of the world brightens my heart during this uncertainty.

The pandemic continues with new variants of the virus spreading. My roommate Jazz caught COVID during Easter 2022, and we celebrated a dinner together on our separate balconies. I went to Mass at Our Lady of Sorrows Parish and saw my friend Jane. We sat together for the liturgy. Unfortunately, I couldn't visit my family because they were worried that I could have been contagious.

I seek peace during this time of upheaval through prayer. I talk to my friends and family frequently to stay connected. Even when I can't do things as planned—like traveling or visiting family more often—I feel calm. I know the Lord is taking care of my needs and I trust in his plan for me.

A pandemic can't stop the abundant goodness that Jesus bestows on his beloved ones. I feel blessed because I have a place to live, a good job to fulfil, and strong family and friend connections.

Now many of the restrictions are being lifted: masks are no longer necessary, restaurants are open, churches at full capacity again. I feel closer to normal as I move through my daily activities of work, dance, shopping, and going to Mass. Continuing my routine and receiving the sacraments gives me courage for the present moment.

Read the story of Jesus' resurrection in Luke 24: 1-12. What do you wonder about in this story?

23. Hope is a muscle we need to exercise

Intense pain from a pinched nerve and muscle spasms in my leg forced me to relinquish my to-do list.

Hot, sharp pain travelled up my leg, and the most comfortable position was lying flat on the floor. Walking became limping. Breathing became a catch-and-release routine. I couldn't even stand to floss my teeth at night.

My sister helped me by cooking dinners, making me laugh, and supporting me on short walks. She showed patience with my constant groans and complaints about how much pain I was in.

My hope was faltering, and I worried that this pain would be my new reality. One night my mom played ukulele over Zoom video as I lay on my back and cried. She let me choose my favourite songs. The next night, we prayed a Rosary together on a video chat. I shifted to find the best sitting position. Her smile lit up my heart. She asked the Lord to show me how much He loves me and that he was suffering with me.

The image of my Saviour suffering alongside me was comforting. I pictured Him holding my hand and squeezing it when a muscle spasm shot fiery shocks up my leg. I let out my breath. Catch and release.

I cancelled story time with my 4-year-old godson because the pain was so strong one night. The next day, we set up a new time to video chat and to my surprise he read me a story. He read *The Cat in the Hat* as I moved now and then to relieve the nerve pain. His bright face beamed with excitement to share his new skill with me.

The Lord was doing a new thing. Stripped of my usual comfort and the busyness of my task list, my priority became peace of heart, and I became aware of how intertwined my mind, body, and spirit are. Amidst hot tears I sang a song I made up, "You can take all this pain away," hoping Jesus would take the hint.

I realized that my identity is not in all the things I do. It's not in what I can offer. It's me and my toothy smile. It's the fact that I was born and am alive. What a miracle: that my parents met, and their parents met. I am a beloved daughter of God.

Accepting my sister's help is difficult sometimes. I don't want to feel like a burden. I am reminded that I am enough. I've read that we are human beings after all, not human doings. We are overcoming. We will always need healing from past wounds and illnesses.

St. Paul says, "For the sake of Christ, then, I am content with weaknesses, insults, hardships, persecutions, and calamities; for when I am weak, then I am strong" (2 Corinthians 12:10).

I have the Lord, and He is everything to me. I trust that He can take care of all things. Even in my suffering, He is there.

I endured pain, and with each discomfort I withstood, I was molded into something new. A strength sprung forth in me. A fierce hope in seeing what is to come. Suffering did not keep my spirits down. Hope is like a muscle. I chose to exercise it more than self-pity.

I will not give up!

I have a compressed disc in my lower back, so I know pain will come again. I will withstand it and learn to move in ways that help it to heal. Physical pain doesn't last forever. Thankfully, I have healing professionals and family who help.

Next time someone asks if you need help, say yes!

24. "Just to be alive is a grand thing"

Daisies and dandelions dotted the grass around my picnic blanket. Shade from tall pine trees created a perfect spot for me to rest in. I kicked off my running shoes and let my bare feet enjoy the cool breeze. Lying down on the blanket, tucked away in Queen Elizabeth Park, I felt like I was in my own piece of paradise. Birds flitted from treetop to tree branch. Fuzzy bees flew by and visited the pink rhododendrons nearby. The smell of ferns and evergreens reminded me of past hiking trips. Hunger pains told me it was nearly dinner time.

Calling my mom, we chatted for a good half hour. After the conversation about our hopes and dreams, we said a short prayer together. Two young girls were sharing snacks on a picnic blanket near me. They laughed and picked up pinecones. I dug into my handbag for my red beaded rosary, a gift from my mom. Sitting with my chin tilted toward the sky, I prayed the Glorious Mysteries with many intentions in my heart.

The Lord is generous in His love. Even with the social isolation brought on by pandemic health measures, I felt community in the many phone calls, text messages, and video chats I shared with my friends and family. We became more creative about how we connected. Virtual dance parties, brunches, movie dates, and Mass became ways to bond when we could not gather in person.

God's love cannot be undone with an outbreak of a virus, even though the pandemic caused my anxiety to rise. It was a "corona coaster" of worries and emotions. Going out in nature and hearing my loved ones' voices over the phone was calming and grounding. I was surprised by my increased desire to create art, bake, dance, and laugh with loved ones.

My dream of completing my book moved to the forefront of my mind. I know that my small plans are nothing to what God has planned for me. His plans are bigger and better than mine. I felt like God would bless my little "yes" in taking action. Without having my social calendar full, I used the extra time to foster my creative pursuits. I felt the Lord say to me in prayer, "Pick up the pen and be brave." I journaled, wrote poems, took notes, and jotted ideas down. As a writer, living life vibrantly fills the well of creativity. I went for many walks, read lots of books, and filled my hours with varied activities that brought material to my writing desk.

Being in an environment that helps me do the work and having the right tools is key. For the longest time, I was without a laptop because my old one crashed. I bought a new one online and had it delivered to my house. Thankfully, I had backed up my files and didn't lose seven years of work on my book.

When we open ourselves up to what we believe God is calling us to, He provides the means. It's amazing how many people He has connected me with to assist me in writing my memoir. "For I, the Lord your God, hold your right hand; it is I who say to you, 'Fear not, I will help you'" (Isaiah 41:13).

The excitement of possibility and leaning into the mystery of God's plan helped me live through the pandemic with hope. I cultivated the garden of my heart, watered it with prayer, acts of love, and faithful trust.

As Agatha Christie said in her autobiography, "I like living. I have sometimes been wildly despairing, acutely miserable, racked with sorrow, but through it all I still know quite certainly that just to be alive is a grand thing."

Create art, bake, dance, or laugh with loved ones.

25. The joy of dancing like nobody's watching

Walking through my neighbourhood, I noticed flowers blooming bright in the gardens, dancing in the wind.

I wondered, *do flowers hide their colour, sultriness, softness, vivaciousness, or beauty?* No, they do not hide. Their brilliant colours shine. Their foliage beams with what they are meant to be. I felt the Lord saying, "You too, let all your colours shine, beam. Do not hide your virtues, talents, and beauty. Do not hide them."

I felt it the night I danced in the moonlight, my sense of hope renewed. Opening the creaky gate covered in ivy and slipping to my dance floor, the alleyway behind the house, I felt a surge of excitement. The perfect spot to move free with form, expression, and passion.

Using the moves of a flamenco dancer, a ballet dancer, and a contemporary dancer, I experienced joy again. After months of searing leg and back pain, my strength returned. My muscles were not pulsing uncomfortably anymore. I could move and breathe. I could dance. For the next couple of weeks, I danced freely in the alley every evening with my music playing.

I tried to recall the choreography I had learned in my dance classes, adding my own flair. The wide-open space was my theatre. I delighted in jumping and twirling with my long hair whipping in the wind. It felt amazing. I was getting stronger.

When I was in the middle of the pain, I thought it would always be that way. I could not see past the discomfort. My prayers asked questions like *What are you trying to teach me, Lord?* And *Can you please take this pain away?* I didn't like suffering, and it felt like there was no end to it. I offered up the pain to God for the benefit of others.

Amazingly, time heals wounds. Slowly, the numbness in my toes disappeared. I could stretch and walk without trouble. Being able to dance again taught me to trust in the Lord's faithfulness. He knows what is in my heart and gently cares for it. My neighbours might not have expected to see me jumping for joy in the alley as they put out their trash and mowed their lawns. But that's exactly what they saw. I danced as if I had just discovered I had legs. An indescribable feeling of lightness and joy.

I am grateful for who God made me and who I am becoming. I haven't always been this free. Healing from any illness takes time. Back pain and bipolar disorder taught me to lean on God and that I am not in control. When I experience pain or my moods move from high to low, I can always rely on God's unchanging love for me.

So, if you find yourself swaying to music, don't be shy. Know that I probably am dancing like a flower in the wind too.

Dance!

26. The prayer in doing chores

While washing dishes with pink gloves in hot suds, I paused to think about all the gifts in my life. The people, the pursuit of a dream, the crafting of a memoir. It all means so much to me. To leave a legacy. To help end stigma. Soap suds squeaked and popped. Plates clattered together. My mind drifted into a hope-filled reverie.

The sun emerged behind rain clouds, and outside the window a bright green canopy of trees lined the street. A newness emerged even during a worldwide pandemic. There was a change in the weather. The smell of lilacs and honeysuckle in the alley wafted into my little grey house.

Leaving the sink, I carried the trash outside and tossed the compost in with a whump. Stretching my arms to the sky, I watched for aviator-like bumblebees passing by. An evening songbird sang high on the telephone wire. The ivy covering the gate trembled in the slight wind. A smile pulled at the corners of my mouth. *I am going to be okay.*

My days are full, and my nights calm. I have peace and joy. The Lord is my all in all. I give myself to Him completely. I even give Him the lost and broken pieces of my heart to find and repair. His love heals me through relationships with my friends and family and time of prayer.

Often, I say, *Jesus, I trust in you. You take care of everything.* Many times, when I have felt invisible, rejected, and lonely, He is with me through it all. I may not be perfect, but I am enough. I am learning to "trust in the slow work of God" and to "give our Lord the benefit of believing that his hand is leading" (Harter).

Sometimes it is difficult to follow the advice from Father Pierre Teilhard de Chardin, SJ, in his short piece "Trust in the Slow Work of God" to "accept the anxiety of feeling yourself in suspense and incomplete" (Harter).

The ordinary task of doing dishes helps me silence the noise that surrounds me and talk to God. I long to speed ahead through the chores and work on my personal projects. I can be impatient. "And yet," says Father de Chardin, "it is the law of progress that it is

made by passing through some stages of instability—
and that it may take a very long time."

The slow growth in relationships and work is almost
unnoticeable. Gradually, with grace and action
new relationships take shape and mature. When I
take a deep breath in nature, I am serene, with life
flourishing all around me. It takes a long time for a
tree to grow tall in a forest and that reminds me of the
steady movement of God in my life. I am present to all
the blessings I have.

Who am I to be loved by a God so great? I am more
aware of His goodness when I reflect on my day with
gratitude. I am grateful for rain-picked raspberries
from my elderly neighbour. Time spent with loved
ones I hadn't seen in months brings such joy. The
beauty of yellow roses and fragrance of jasmine
flowers in nearby gardens are lovely.

"O give thanks to the Lord, for he is good, for his
mercy endures forever" (Psalm 136:1). Instead of
dreading chores, I relish the time to clean. Finding
restoration in the Lord who is with me through it all.

Complete a chore you have been avoiding with gratitude.

27. Gifts and crosses

I woke up in a foul mood. Noise interrupted my weekend sleep. My afternoon plans were cancelled. I had a heated and tearful conversation with my brother. A low mood settled on me at lunch. My day crashed down like my internet connection.

After crying in my room for a bit, I joined my sister and her boyfriend to walk to the beach. My spirits sank like a shipwreck. I needed to do something fast. As we were walking, a Wendy's sign appeared. In an instant, I craved a Frosty. I said goodbye to my sister and her boyfriend and lined up for a chocolate dessert. Tucking the icy treat in my bag, I walked the rest of the way to a park near the ocean.

I looked around for shade. Many people had the same goal. I walked around thinking I might have to bake in the hot sun. To my delight, I spotted a tiny pine tree in the middle of the dried grass. I spread out my blanket and wiped sweat from the back of my neck. The tree sheltered my face as I dug into my Frosty with a spoon.

Only a part of it had melted in the heat. The light chocolate flavour glided down my throat, and I relished the moment. After I ate, I felt sleepy and rested in the shade. Pine needles brushed my hair, and the heat felt like a soft blanket on my skin. I dozed to the sound of seagulls calling and bike wheels whizzing by me. Peace washed over me as I rested. I felt like a solar panel recharging in the afternoon sun.

Bipolar disorder has offered me the opportunity to gain new skills in navigating ups and downs. As a woman, I already experience natural changes in energy, mood, and behaviour throughout the month; bipolar disorder brings additional challenges. At times I have boundless energy for multiple projects and social activities. But then a few days later, I want to crawl into a ball of blankets and just sip coffee, away from it all. It is humbling and draining.

The expectations I place on myself are part of the challenge. I always expect my performance to be amazing, and when it isn't, I want to escape. I want to leave sadness behind me. But even nature has seasons.

Now, I see the sadness was signalling to me.

You matter. Take the time to do your creative work. You are worth it. Let the pen hit the paper and twirl.

Just being alive is enough. There is nothing you need to prove. Don't give up.

The words of Talia Kruse, a Catholic mental health coach, resonate with me. She says, "The Lord gave me gifts, and the Lord has given me crosses – but both are to be offered up for his glory. He gave me the gift of being driven, and motivated, but he also gave me this cross of bipolar disorder which in many ways disrupts these gifts. Why would he give me such contradicting attributes? Only he knows – perhaps for my humility, perhaps for me to realize that not all things are easy. Whatever the case is, he knows and is faithful."

Every up and down with bipolar disorder teaches me something new about the faithfulness of God. He doesn't give up on me. "With him, I do not feel alone, or useless or abandoned, but involved in a plan of salvation that one day will lead to paradise" (Pope John Paul I).

Feel your emotions and know they rise and fall.

28. When life goes up in smoke, keep a sense of humour, kindness, and grit

I woke to the sound of whirring helicopters circling my neighbourhood. My first thought was, *Oh no, not another SWAT team stakeout.*

My sister was already eating breakfast. "Can you check the news and see what's happening?" I asked her while rushing to put on a fresh pot of coffee.

As I dressed and got ready for work, my sister read out the news. "There has been a fire at King Edward and Cambie. Five businesses on the east side of Cambie were destroyed. The blaze started at 3 a.m. in the morning behind the café. The main intersection is closed going all directions. They safely removed the cats boarding above the sushi restaurant."

Each time she read something about the fire, I said, "Oh no. Oh no." It was so sad.

The QE Park walk-in clinic and pharmacy were the two businesses I will miss the most. The owner of the pharmacy and her assistant knew me by name and took care of me. When I had trouble describing what I needed, they guessed correctly. Two weeks before the fire, they asked if I needed a flu shot and fit me in between appointments so I could get it right away. They were caring and kind. I will miss them.

The day after the fire, I looked at the ruins with my sister. The smell of smoke from the charred remains of the buildings reminded me how temporary things are and that life can change in an instant. Even my hope in God could be extinguished if I do not live a life of ordered love.

Father Francis Fernandez says, in the fifth volume of *In Conversations with God*, "If we live with Christ close by our side we will need few possessions in order to be happy as children of God."

Reflecting on the loss from the recent fire sparked a resolve to live without regret and shook me awake to realize that life moves on, whether or not you are ready.

I was born with a sense of humour, kindness, and grit. These qualities help me cope with the unexpected anxieties that come my way: the battle to find balance with a mood disorder; grieving deceased friends, family members, and dear ones; the interior struggle towards holiness.

I have a King who dotes on me. He heals me again and again. I trust He has a heaven of wellness planned for me. I often imagine walking with Jesus in a garden. He shows me new delights, tall sunflowers, and a vineyard in bloom.

There will be things that upset us and make us worry. The Lord didn't promise us an easy life but one full of joy. With our eyes resting on Him, we can trust He will take care of us. "I came that they may have life, and have it abundantly," says the Lord (John 10:10).

Will you see only the ashes from a fire? Or a sweet offering to begin again and offer everything to the Lord? My sadness at the loss of the relationships at the pharmacy has brought me to a place of wonder.

What can God do with the impossible? What can I do to live more? What am I meant to do in this life? If I don't have long to live, I don't want to wait to do what I can do now. As Jesus said, "Let your loins be girded and your lamps burning" (Luke 12:35).

Only God can fill my heart with the fullness of love. In this disorienting time, I need to orient back to the true north. I return my gaze to the Lord who is my

Arise Shine & Live

comfort. May He continue to pour His love into my heart, and yours.

Spend some time in prayer at a church or in your home.

29. Prayer of a "silly woman in front of the tabernacle"

Early one workday morning, I knelt in the chapel in our building. The sanctuary lamp flickered and glowed in the dark, a tangible reminder that Jesus was there with me listening to my prayers.

I watched the candle flame dance, its light shining, and felt a peace wash over me. The warmth settled like a wool shawl around my shoulders. I am never alone even when I can't see the candle burning.

My prayer went something like this: *Please go with me. I am a silly woman in front of the tabernacle trying to find healing and strength. Lord, I know You can help me and all my dear ones. You are silent and strong. I know when everything goes wrong, You are right beside me. Hold me close to You. Never let me fear. I want to be one with You. I love you, my dear Saviour. I am worried, but I put all my worries in your hands.*

Arise Shine & Live

Sometimes, when I pray, I can hear a quiet voice, "Darling, look upon me. Do not be afraid. I am always with you. I will not abandon you. I delight in your efforts, tenacity, and smiles. Do not weary. I will carry you when you are tired. I love you. You are mine. My daughter, be brave."

After those precious quiet minutes, I picked up my lunch kit and went upstairs to my desk, ready to offer my day for my loved ones. I set out to work in a manner pleasing to God and my colleagues. Each phone call, email, and written report is an opportunity for prayer.

Even if you are a student and have a lot of studying to do, it can be a time of prayer. I often think about my writing. When it seems like I can't take time away from chores or other pressing work, I remind myself that writing is also a way to pray.

I am my biggest critic. When I see my finished work—either my writing, podcast, or videos—I start to point out all that I did wrong. Or when I fall into the same sins again and again.

I turn to the Lord saying, *Lord, I am your cracked clay pot. I am your unpolished art. Mould me and fashion me.*

The beauty of that moment is that I can begin again. I learn from my mistakes. I grow and adapt and change. I lean on the strength of the Lord in prayer and the sacraments and practising flexibility. I desire to be ready for the Lord like those wise bridesmaids who had extra oil for their lamps.

I had trouble sleeping for a whole week. My mental illness and stress caused sensory hallucinations. The symptoms passed, and I learned that taking the rest I need is non-negotiable to stay healthy. I treasure the hours of solid sleep.

When I find myself concerned about something in the news, I hold on to the word of God. I look to the things that I can control, which are my "thoughts, muscles and impulses" (Low). The peace I receive when I read Scripture and give my burdens to the Lord amazes me. It does help!

I continue to rise each morning and give my best. Some days, I am more tired than others. I focus on what I can do and "be like the fox who makes more tracks than necessary, some in the wrong direction. Practice resurrection" (Berry).

Offer a prayer while doing your chores for your loved ones.

30. Redesign your living space and unclutter your mind for Jesus

"Let's move the little blue couch over there!" My sister pointed to the wall close to the kitchen.

I nodded. "That could work."

After watching a few episodes of the *Design Doctors,* we drew a new floor plan for our sitting room. We were tired of the layout of our room, which we spent more time in since the beginning of the pandemic. We looked at the five points of focus in interior design: light, space, colour, flow, and storage.

The piano now had pride of place with plants and lighting around it. We moved our dark furniture to be next to each other creating warmth. Our white armchairs had decorative pillows and a blanket draped over them, one for each of us to curl up in. We rearranged what was on our bookshelves, donating items we no longer use.

Using creative design in our home helped me have a new perspective on personal projects. Rearranging, culling, and cleaning uncluttered my head space as well. I no longer felt stuck. I had options. I can restart, reformat, and redo what doesn't work in writing. I can refresh, renew, and restore relationships.

When my prayer life dried up, I remembered that Jesus takes pride of place in my heart. I needed to toss all the useless junk and sin that clutters up my soul.

"We need to be reminded that every second of our survival does really mean that we are new from God's fingers, so that it requires no more than the miracle which we never notice to restore to us our virgin-heart at any moment we like to choose," wrote Caryll Houselander in *The Reed of God*.

I opened the window to let the cold winter air in. We admired our work, and I danced in the wide-open space in the centre of the room. This room was now *hygge*—the Danish word for coziness, comfort, and contentment. Candlelight really makes the home *hyggelig* (hygge-like).

We can open our hearts for Jesus to find an inviting sitting room. Oh, how I want him to be with me during the sometimes-dreary season of winter.

January can be a very blue month for me. The dark days are a struggle. With a fresh look in my home, I have a gift of change and an eagerness for what the new year will bring. When I have hopes, dreams, and goals that I am anticipating, my life has purpose.

I like to pray the Catholic Christian Outreach apostle's prayer. It goes like this: "... Lord, I will go anywhere you want me to go, I will do anything you want me to do, and I will say anything you want me to say."

Then I step out in faith: loving the people in my life, moving forward in writing my books, and showing up at work to serve. I know that the Lord loves a cheerful giver. Someone willing to be His instrument. He has a plan for me. It thrills me and worries me at the same time.

What if I don't measure up? What if I mess things up?

Moses did not reach the promised land because he did not entrust himself to the Lord. It's not easy to do. Daily, I need to choose to trust in my King and my God. I need to believe in His majesty and mercy. I want Him to be comfortable in the depths of my heart.

Receiving the sacrament of confession is like interior design for my soul. I have been seeking reconciliation, which cleans out my heart. Holding onto the promise of freedom from my sin, I begin again.

Houselander writes, "The question which most people will ask is: 'Can someone whose life is already cluttered up with trivial things get back to this virginal emptiness? Of course he can; if a bird's nest has been filled with broken glass and rubbish, it can be emptied.'"

Jesus will see me through the winter blues. I may not always feel his presence, but I trust that he is with me on the little blue couch in my heart.

Look for a way to rearrange or change something about your living space to make it cozier.

31. When your heart dips low, turn to Jesus

The setting sun reflected light—orange, yellow, red, and blue—in the glass high rises we drove past. The winding, tree-lined road trees looked softer in the evening light. After days of rain, my sister and I went for a drive to get out of the house. I needed a change in routine. Our goal was to get to Burnaby Mountain Park before sunset. We listened to music and chatted as the light in the sky warmed to a golden glimmer.

After taking a detour, we finally made it to the top. When I looked around at the view of mountains, ocean, sky, and the twinkling city lights, I exhaled. This unique sunset reminded me that any suffering or stressful situation will pass with time. Tall evergreens framed my photos as I tried to capture the moment.

Enroute, I hoped to get to my desired distraction—this peach-tinted landscape—before the sun had vanished. Taking a moment to watch the clouds drift by and the lights on the bridge twinkle helped me relax. I wondered what tomorrow would bring.

Eagerness was a word I chose to describe that year, because I had so many things to look forward to, including an end to the restriction on visiting friends and family due to the coronavirus.

I missed hugging my parents and siblings. My nephew was growing so fast, and photos and videos were all I had to witness it. My friends and I chatted on the phone often but it didn't replace the comfort of their presence. I felt empty and isolated.

Spending quality time with my friends and family changed. Sending and receiving rapid text messages with multiple emojis expressing sentiments is good. They helped me to stay connected. But I desired to be in the same room as my loved ones. I was lonely.

Holding hands and sharing hugs, laughs, and smiles are such wonderful treasures. Helen Keller said, "Although, the world is full of suffering, it is full also of the overcoming of it." Each day, I prayed we were getting closer to being together again.

While reading the Bible one night, words from the Gospel of Luke jumped off the page at me. "Blessed are you who are poor, for yours is the kingdom of God. Blessed are you who are hungry now, for you will be filled. Blessed are you who weep now, for you will laugh" (Luke 6:20).

I felt poor in spirit. I hungered for hope in the future. I wept in sadness. Through it all, Jesus blessed me with his undying friendship.

The intimacy I experience in my relationship with Him can't be restricted. When my heart dips low, I turn to Jesus by spending time in prayer. I only wish that He could wrap His arms around me in a big hug. I felt blessed to receive hugs from my sister, who was also my roommate. I feel like I can never get enough.

Standing on the hill in the wintry cold with my sister, I felt a sense of wonder. I vowed to remember God's promises when I feel scared. I turned around and saw the moon rising, its edges faded.

"Want to pray a Rosary?"

My sister and I sat in the warm car as the sky darkened. After offering up our intentions, we prayed together, our eyes watching the final glow of the sunset.

"Hail Mary, full of grace ..."

Reciting the familiar prayers, I was amazed at the feeling of peace that grew stronger in me. In this calm mood, I could enjoy what I had and be satisfied. When we finished the Rosary, we drove away and that feeling remained. What I know for certain is that I am cared for, and so are you. Our heavenly Father loves us. Love always remains.

Find something of beauty to enjoy: music, a sunset, art etc.

32. Riches are in relationships

Margaretha, my 90-year-old neighbour, called me every day after I told her I wasn't feeling well.

Her concern felt like a grandmother's would.

My grandparents passed away years ago. I only knew two of them. My paternal grandpa was sick in a hospital when I was a little girl. I remember holding his soft, wrinkled hands as the nurses fed him, but I don't remember his funeral because I was so young. "Mimi" is what we called my maternal grandma. She lived with us during my childhood and teen years.

There is something special about the love of grandparents. I miss them. I wish I knew the two I never met.

Margaretha was happy to hear from me when I called her on my lunch break.

"Good thing it was nothing serious. Yeah, I worry."

We chatted about her trip to Canadian Tire with her son. She bought bulbs to plant in her garden, a new variety that grows tall like hollyhocks.

"My wood-burning stove isn't working anymore. Something is wrong with the pipe."

"Are you going to fix it?"

"No, John says we could get a gas fireplace."

Pre-COVID, my sister and I visited her house. We brought our ukuleles, and Margaretha welcomed us with tea and cookies. The whole room smelled of wood smoke and roasting onions.

Having an elderly neighbour care about you is like having a grandparent giving you a hug. We always talk about the weather because if it's raining it means she can't go out in her garden. She grew up working on a farm in Germany, so she is tireless, despite her arthritic knees. Margaretha always tends to the garden that surrounds her home, even when she is in pain.

I was grateful for her reliable phone calls checking in to see how I was doing during the pandemic. Talking to her makes me want to trust the Lord more. He always sends me love in the way I need.

God provides for me when I am feeling depressed or overwhelmed. Sometimes I need to wail and cry in His presence, to know that He is present in this pain, worry, and fear. If I take time for silent prayer, reading Scripture, and a good spiritual book, He is waiting for me there. His peace warms my heart. I bask in the joy of knowing I am his beloved daughter.

When I am full of God, I can reach out to my loved ones and be present to their needs. "Riches are in relationships, not possessions," says Jane Trufant Harvey in *Ask Him, Simple Words to Jumpstart Your Conversation with God*.

My phone rang on the weekend, and I couldn't pick it up in time.

"Hello, Lisa, it's Margaretha. How are you? I miss you. Come over." I was sad during that difficult time when we couldn't visit people's houses. It was difficult to accept that I could not visit Margaretha in person. I did what I could and called her instead.

Our divine call to holiness is through the life of our family. Ordinary phone calls, visits, and conversations bring supernatural love to our relationships. As Margaretha nurtures the plants in her garden, I am going to set down strong roots to rise and grow in love.

I entrust the Lord with my life. I can't do anything on my own strength. I am a child in His arms. He is taking care of me, as He is taking care of you. We share our struggles and help each other.

As Thomas Merton says, "Love is our true destiny. We do not find the meaning of life by ourselves alone – we find it with another. We do not discover the secret of our lives merely by study and calculation in our isolated meditations. The meaning of our life is a secret that has to be revealed to us in love."

Take the opportunity to call a friend or visit them.

33. Walking in the garden with God

Tall bamboo stalks swayed and light filtered through the trees as I walked through the VanDusen Botanical Garden. A sanctuary of trees: red cedars and paperbark maples, all reaching to the heavens.

I was visiting the garden and walking its winding paths to look for new growth. Lenten roses, *Helleborus orientalis*, were one of the garden's many varieties. I took photos of floating blooms in a bowl of water during one of my frequent visits.

Natural beauty, a vision of God's creativity, brings me joy.

Walking has become one of my favourite self-care tools in my mental health recovery kit. I go for short walks on lunch breaks in the many nearby parks and gardens near my office. I've learned that when I move it improves my mood.

One lunch hour in the garden, a Canada goose came up from behind and honked at me. Luckily, I had finished eating my fettuccine. I packed up and moved out of his way. He may have been hungry, but I had nothing to give him.

Listening to the birds calling from the trees around me, I smiled. God cares for us more than a goose, or a sparrow. He takes care of us all.

I can walk, run, and dance. It's an exhilarating feeling to move in my body. God designed my body to be an image of him, and I see God's beauty in the diversity of my own family.

While walking, I find renewed clarity, creative ideas flow, and my muscles stretch after sitting for long hours. When I walk with my sister or a friend, the conversation flows with our breath. As the season changes, it is calming and refreshing to be outside. I love watching the light lengthen in spring evenings. Sunsets fill the sky with colours I want to imitate on canvas.

Being in nature, I imagine what it would have been like for Adam and Eve to walk with God in the Garden of Eden. Our story is also about walking in the garden with God.

Do we leave space for Him to be with us?

...rite Him into our hearts?

...we ask Him to light our path?

Often, I picture myself walking in a garden with Jesus. His sandals are tossed aside, and His bare feet lead the way through a vineyard. Jesus reaches out to pick a grape, checking its ripeness. I follow beside Him, watching His every move. We pass a cluster of trees, and I point out to Jesus that it's a great spot for a picnic. He smiles at me. I promise to spend more time with Him.

During Lent, I reflect on how Jesus desired His disciples to keep watch and pray with Him in the Garden of Olives. He was exhausted and needed emotional and spiritual support from His closest friends. Contemplating His passion, I am so grateful for His suffering, dying, and rising. Even though His disciples failed to keep watch, Jesus loved them. His loyalty and love are something to imitate.

I want to be close to the Lord and know his plans for me. I feel closer to him when I pray, even if I can't hear his audible voice. I know he hears me.

When stress seeps into my thoughts, I look for words of truth and hope in Scripture. As a writer, words hold great significance to me. Reading holy Scripture is a soothing balm on my heart, as comforting as walking with a friend.

As Proverbs says, "Trust in the Lord with all your heart, and do not lean on your own understanding. In all your ways acknowledge him, and he will make straight your paths" (3:5-6).

Action leads to purpose, and I'm lacing up my shoes and hoping that with each next step I take I walk in God's way for me.

Pick a book that is spiritually nourishing to meditate on.

34. Making use of therapy, sleep, and a good dose of laughter

Walking home from work one day, the coat buckle on my sleeve caught in a fence as I tried to move out of someone's way. Because of my fast pace, I was pulled back sharply, and my leg flew up. I let out a big, "Oh!"

I smiled at myself and let go of the embarrassment. As I walked the rest of the way home, I chuckled quietly at how funny I must have looked.

I don't take myself too seriously, which helps me laugh easily. I enjoy giggling with my sisters, brothers, and friends. To have a hearty chuckle—the one that comes deep from within my belly—is the best feeling.

I take laughing seriously. It is a wellness strategy I love to tap into.

I took an online improv class with Tiffani Sierra from *Improv It Up* during the first wave of the pandemic. We were a small group of individuals engaging with the power of our voice and actions. We participated in games to increase our confidence in acting with strangers.

One game was to come up with a very ordinary skill that we were good at and turn it into a superhero name. My name for the game was the Ultimate Compost Emptier. We added an action as we shared our name with an epic voice. I felt silly and strong at the same time.

Tiffani shared how improvisation can help our mental health flourish. In her acting classes with businesses, youth, and communities people experience more freedom in expressing themselves.

The improv attitude is to accept things the way they are and do something to improve the situation. It's the "Yes, and" approach.

In my neighbourhood, one homeowner posted a sign that read, "Silly walks," on their fence – a nod to the Monty Python sketch "The Ministry of Silly Walks."

I lifted my leg high and started hopping along. I couldn't do it without laughing, and my sister laughed along with me. That street became part of my route when I needed to do errands. Each time I walked by that house I invented a new silly walk. It was so much fun!

Living with seasons of depression, which are often accompanied with suicidal thoughts, I have come to treasure the simple joys of life. My mood disorder leads me through many hills and valleys. Sometimes, I experience intense sadness and have a difficult time holding onto hope. When I am on a downward spiral, I reach out to those around me.

My family is always there for me. Encouraging me and listening to my worries. Their support makes me want to share the joy I have. I can relate to Robin Williams' words, "I think the saddest people always try their hardest to make people happy. Because they know what it's like to feel absolutely worthless and they don't want anybody else to feel like that."

I make use of all the help that God has provided for me: therapy, medicine, sleep, and a good dose of laughter.

In his *Apostolic Exhortation on Christian Joy*, Pope Paul VI wrote, "to savour in a simple way the many human joys that the Creator places in our path: the elating joy of existence and of life; the joy of chaste and sanctified love; the peaceful joy of nature and silence; the sometimes austere joy of work well done; the joy and satisfaction of duty performed; the transparent joy of purity, service and sharing; the demanding joy of sacrifice."

Savouring the simple human joys is a way to stay in the present moment. With God there is unending joy.

Nothing can take away the joy in my heart, which is Jesus. He is the source of all joy. When I start to feel sad, I recall all the blessings I have. "This day is holy to our Lord. Do not grieve, for the joy of the LORD is your strength" (Nehemiah 8:10).

Will you laugh a little more knowing that in Jesus your joy will be complete?

Enjoy a comedy or go to an improv show where there is bound to be laughter.

35. You're not a robot

I am not a robot.

I have emotions, a heart, an intellect, and a will. I learned that "feelings are not facts" from the cognitive behavioural techniques of Dr. Abraham Low. Even so, feelings can indicate truth to us: how we feel in a situation, where we need support, or our need to find peace.

My colleague Sandy Marshall, Associate Superintendent of the Catholic Independent Schools of Vancouver Archdiocese, shared her prayer time reflections with me recently. Staff of the superintendent's office gather every morning at 9 a.m. to pray together. Taking turns to lead the prayer, we pray a decade of the Rosary for each staff member during their birthday month, for deceased members of our community, and those who need healing.

We stand at our cubicles or our office doors—spaced out due to COVID safety restrictions—and yet we are still united. I noticed Sandy facing towards her office window as she sat in her chair. Her window overlooks a beautiful view of our office's Vancouver neighbourhood.

Sandy said that she focuses on the trees and then on the houses and buildings. She calls it her "I am not a robot" game, inspired by the online test to purchase tickets or to log into a website: when a site asks you to click on the boxes with cars or bridges or fire hydrants, and once you answer correctly, you have proven you are not a robot.

As someone who deals with anxiety and panic attacks, techniques that bring me back to the present moment are helpful. Sandy created her own mindfulness practice with her window reflections. Her exercise inspired me to think about all the things that I have learned to help my mental health.

I have found practical wisdom in mindfulness exercises. Dr. Gregory Bottaro talks about trusting in God more and finding peace in his book, *The Mindful Catholic: Finding God One Moment at a Time*. We could all use a little more peace.

I often need reminders to bring my thoughts back to the present moment, when I get caught in thinking traps and forget that God is taking care of me.

I work in an office that celebrates growing spiritually, intellectually, and relationally. It is a blessing to work with people who follow Steve Farber's motto, expressed in *The Radical Edge*: "Do what you love in the service of people who love what you do."

Sandy is one of my mentors in work and in life. As Nick Schneider, Director of Finance, said, "Everything you say is quotable." Sandy's attention to the little things is inviting, like how she decorates a prayer centre for each liturgical season in our office. She is someone I turn to for recipes, party décor ideas, and how to gather a room.

What I love about the mission of the CISVA is its task is to "develop as balanced persons spiritually, emotionally, physically and intellectually." The Lord grants us the natural means to heal and grow. I have recently begun eating healthier with a delicious array of vegetables, protein, and grains. The Lord provides everything we need to live well.

Don't dismiss practical help like medicines, therapy, and other secular resources in favour of praying harder for healing. God provides us the means to find peace, health, and wellness. We are human. Our energy fluctuates, and we need time to rest too.

Prayer is a gift of time to rest in God's presence. Finding the balance of our priorities is an ongoing journey. As St. Faustina wrote in her diary, "My one occupation is to live in the presence of my Heavenly Father."

Find a healthy recipe for dinner.

36. All shall be well

Sunshine floods the coffee shop through the floor-to-ceiling windows as I lick chocolate chip cookie crumbs from my fingers.

I often overbook myself, not leaving time to just be and create. This weekend I walked in the sunshine through Vancouver neighbourhoods and found a quiet place to pen a few poems. Creative time alone is essential for me as a writer. I need solitude to think and let words pour on to the computer screen or journal at hand.

I read the messages on Matchstick Coffee Roasters' cookie wrapper:

"We don't have all the answers, but we do have pastry."

"Life can be complicated. Take a moment to yourself and enjoy what is, or maybe what was, in this bag. We hope it brings you the nourishment (and pause) you need."

Arise Shine & Live

In times of sadness and fatigue I often have no words. The first weeks and months of the pandemic were challenging, and the news more distressing as each week passed.

In order not to lose heart during difficult times, I look to the sacraments, where Jesus pours his love into me. Confession is a source of renewal for me that I return to again and again. While attending daily Mass, I recommit myself to God. In adoration I let the Lord shine his light on me.

Sometimes healing looks like taking a nap. I lie down and tuck the covers under my chin. I adjust my eye mask and close my eyes. It feels so good as sleep comes over me, rosary beads in hand. I don't have to be afraid. Mama Mary, as I like to call her, offers protection and prayers answered. And wherever Mary is, Jesus promises that he is here with me too. I trust Him. He is a faithful God. Warm waves of comfort expand across my whole body. I whisper, "Come, Lord Jesus."

The house is quiet as I wake.

I say to myself, *Just be. Do not worry about the things you need to do tomorrow. My work is never finished. If I don't take time to restore, I will always feel exhausted.*

Even better than perfect words spoken at the right time has been the presence of my friends and family during times of trial. My cousin Sarah rides her bike to meet me, bringing her French bulldog in her backpack. His ears flap and his tongue wags. Oakley has been my favourite furry companion since the day he rested his head on my knee when I told Sarah I wanted cuddles. A wagging tail greets everyone Oakley meets. He is not afraid to show his brokenness, his scoliosis and one eye. I have seen him run with a limp in a race and cheered him on even though he ran in the wrong direction. I think that is what makes him dear to me.

When I am experiencing the symptoms of bipolar disorder, I remind myself that it is not my fault. The illness comes and goes in periods of stress.

"All shall be well, and all shall be well, and all manner of things shall be well," said Julian of Norwich, who lived in isolation and survived a pandemic when the black death swept through Europe between 1348-50 and again between 1361-62.

She experienced suffering and through it all wrote words of wisdom and hope. Her writing inspires me to continue my own work, to take the time for my craft amid the suffering and uncertainty around me.

Sitting on a picnic blanket with my cousin and Oakley or in my living room, I know that I am loved.

Our greatest contribution to the world is the attention, encouragement, and love that we give each other. We can give these things every day, and these gifts don't cost us money.

Ecclesiastes famously said, "For everything there is a season, and a time for every matter under the heaven" (Ecclesiastes 3:1). There is a time for solitude and a time to be together.

I recently bought my cousin Sarah the children's book *Can I Sit with You?* by Sarah Jacoby. It is a story about a little dog who wants to be with his owner, a growing girl, in all the happy and sad moments of her life.

Companionship is a gift, to be both received and given.

I don't walk alone in this life. No one does. It is in difficult times that community matters. The presence of another makes a difference. It can save a life.

Who will you sit with today?

Reach out to a friend.

37. Choose an attitude of hope

Splashing my toes and stretching my arms past my head, I smiled and breathed in the warm summer air. Stress washed away in the spray as I threw the frisbee and then swam to catch it. Not even the pesky Canadian geese trying to eat our cherries bothered me.

Surrounded by trees on the shore, boats bobbing on the water, and seagulls soaring over the docks, I felt a deep peace. But our external environment alone cannot bring us interior freedom. It is our thoughts that make us feel at ease.

In moments of sheer delight, I forget I have a diagnosis of a chronic mental illness. Floating on my back in Cultus Lake during a weekend getaway, I felt free to be.

An attitude of hope can help us appreciate living each day as a gift.

Viktor Frankl's classic memoir of surviving a concentration camp, *Man's Search for Meaning*, observes that some prisoners who held on to hope to be free one day in the future lived to see it come to pass. Others thought they would be free at Christmas, but when it did not come to be, they gave up and died.

"Everything can be taken from a man but one thing: the last of the human freedoms – to choose one's attitude in any given set of circumstances, to choose one's own way" (Frankl).

I used to think and speak to myself with hurtful words. My self-worth was linked to my diagnosis and how people treated me.

Bipolar disorder was a glaring label that I thought would limit everything about my life and future. *What could I ever be good at if I suffered with suicidal thoughts and felt numb from medicine?*

The depression, weight gain, loss of friends, and dropping out of college pained me. I am a dreamer, and this experience was a nightmare.

I decided to find a way to become whole again the day I received the diagnosis. In the hospital, I complied with the nurses and calmed patients who were trying to escape the locked ward. I even entertained them with origami soccer ball games I made up. On daily walks to get exercise, I learned to hope again. I began to look at the diagnosis as something to solve.

"When we are no longer able to change a situation, we are challenged to change ourselves," Frankl writes. I wanted to step out of the shadows and into the light. *Here I am. It's Lisa!*

I delight in the warmth of friendship. I had not seen my dear friend for a year, so it was extra special to finally catch up in person. Staying at her home for the weekend and spending quality time at the lake was a blessing I will cherish.

My friends never look at me as "less than" or "troubled." They love me for who I am—completely—illness and all. I have received healing and learned to love who I am and who I am created to be.

I am blessed to offer up any mental suffering whether for my loved ones, souls in purgatory, or the whole wide world. I can offer this passive mortification to the Lord in prayer.

I see now, having lived with bipolar disorder for more than a decade, that what is painful can also lead to refinement.

"So that the genuineness of your faith—being more precious than gold that, though perishable, is tested by fire—may be found to result in praise and glory and honour when Jesus Christ is revealed" (1 Peter 1:7).

It took many years to have the courage to share my story with new friends. In prayer, I kept hearing Jesus tell me not to be afraid.

"Be brave!"

I hold on to my hope, my dearest friend, Jesus. I do not have to produce, perform, prove, or please to be worthy.

His love called me out of the shadows. He encourages me to take time to jump in the lake and swim. "My grace is sufficient for you, for power is made perfect in weakness" (2 Corinthians 12:9).

Can you use your courage in a conversation or an activity?

38. Writing as a form of prayer and healing

"You mean you are going to have another kid?"

"Yes," said Mr. and Mrs. Randall.

"Well then," replied Kathy, "Well then, I'll just go and pack up."

"No, Kathy," said Mrs. Randall, "Don't do that. You don't know what the baby will be like."

Excerpt from "A New Baby," a story I wrote at eight years of age.

I recently rediscovered my handwritten stories that survived a house fire. Rereading them, I laughed and cried. I felt such appreciation for little Lisa. The humour and simplicity of the stories triggered memories of childhood. When I was eight years old, I already knew I wanted to be an author when I grew up.

Arise Shine & Live

I look back on these stories with wonder. I wrote about what I knew, and what I had been reading as a child. In the afternoons, I would sit cross-legged in a t-shirt and shorts on the living room floor and write these short stories with my pencil onto scrap paper.

A few of the titles were "A New Baby" (quoted above), "A Surprise Party," and "Fluffy," a story about a classroom pet. They were stories about welcoming new siblings and struggling with math homework. About the joy of an unexpected pet duck, conflict with classmates, and the wish for a surprise party that included the whole school.

When they drove up the driveway her mother knew every little thing to know about Fluffy.

"Well," said her mom, getting out of the car, "I guess I better get a snack for you two."

Excerpt from "Fluffy"

These precious stories remind me that I have always been a writer. When imposter syndrome shows up, I can silence the thoughts that tell me to give up. Writing was something I do for fun. I have always enjoyed spending time with a notebook and pen or reading a book.

"In that moment I remembered again," recalls Sarah Clarkson in *Book Girl*, "that a woman who reads is a woman who ponders, who knows the holy secret of time spent in quiet, the power that comes from stepping back from the madness of screen and email, schedule and headline, to seek an inner place of hush in which she may know her own heart and the voice of the Holy Spirit afresh."

Today, writing is both fun and necessary for healing. At first, I struggled to write about my mental illness. I am thankful for the handful of people who went before me, showing it was possible. I thought, *If they can share their journey, so can I.*

I am not alone. I repeat this to myself often because I can feel so alone. I know I'm not the only one who feels this way at times.

When I got sick as a teenager, I felt alone.

When I received a diagnosis of a chronic mental illness, I felt alone.

When I experience sensory hallucinations, I'm the only one who can see or feel them.

But I am never alone.

Jesus is beside me in times of loneliness and fear. When I feel hopeless, I reach for His love. Sometimes the only vocal prayer I can articulate is "Help!" or "Jesus!"

Mother Mary and all the saints surround me in a heavenly community. I need only lift my thoughts towards them, and the spirit groans out a prayer for help. Many saints experienced mental illness too, which helps me see that holiness is possible for anyone.

My brain works differently than others. Bipolar disorder affects my thoughts, mood, and behaviour, and causes periods of high energy that can lead to a crash of depression if I don't regain balance.

I am learning about presence versus performance. The Lord is patient with me. He loves me even amidst my stumbling and striving. I am buoyed up by His love in the sacraments of reconciliation and the Mass.

Often, I sit in His presence in the chapel and tears form my prayer. Jesus knows exactly what my tears mean, and they bring healing in their release.

He comforts me when I recall the Scripture: "I am with you always" (Matthew 28:20).

My identity as a child of God is a great gift that brings solace in the face of depression. The Lord promises to never abandon me. God gives us our identity, and illness does not define us. We are images of the Creator. God saw that it was good.

Even from the broken parts of my life, newness and transformation can take place.

Writing is a form of prayer too. I speak to the Lord in prayerful letters that give me space to pause and reflect on my needs and the good in my life.

Every word I write about the pain in my past or present lets in light to the suffering parts of my heart. I know that every poem, piece of prose, or fictional story I create is a way to heal from suffering. I embrace the process.

The short stories of my youth motivate me to continue to become the author I have always dreamed of being.

Remember an activity that you loved as a child and reflect on it.

39. Any storm can be weathered

Standing in first position, feet grounded on my soft mat and sunshine on my face, I felt the quiet release of stress.

I dug into my toolkit for a self-care technique to help find balance during a period of mania. The motion of dancing improves my emotions. As part of living with chronic mental illness, I must pay attention to my moods and emotions.

Dancing is one of my passions. I have taken lessons on many styles of dance—hip-hop, flamenco, ballroom, and ballet—as I learned to move my muscles in new ways to get rid of extra energy or monthly blues.

When I dance or exercise, endorphins are released, causing positive feelings. It can feel like I flipped a switch in my brain to recalibrate. Thankfully, dancing is very effective.

This summer, I joined an outdoor ballet class seeking happy chemicals to find inner calm. Suzy Q, ballerina and founder of The Ballet Lounge, brought a spirit of joy and acceptance to our class. Her little dog Gizmo accompanied her and cheered us on. His fluffy little body leaned against my knees as I pet his silky fur. His presence soothed me and made me smile.

Reaching my arms above my head, I embraced the joy of dancing by the sea. I felt connected body and soul. In my mind, I gave over my worries to Jesus.

Finding the beach ballet class was a sign of hope for me. A way to tenderly care for my body and soul.

We are integrated beings. When we calm one part of our bodies and mind, the rest follows suit.

At times, my moods surge up and down like a sailboat tossed at sea. To survive the choppy waves, I need to take down the sails, put a life jacket on, and let the storm pass.

Jesus' love is my constant. His comfort for me shows up, hidden, in the everyday: smiles from friends, cuddles from little Gizmo the ballet dog, and reading the perfect Scripture verse.

We all carry scars and have our own mountains to climb. Jesus whispers to me, "I've got you." He can endure any storm.

I whisper back to Jesus, *I trust in you.*

He calls us to take up our cross and follow Him. These are beautiful words, but to take up the uncomfortable and frustrating circumstances of my life is a challenge I face daily.

Carrying my cross on my own was never the plan. I need Jesus to shoulder it with me. It humbled me to ask for His help.

He surely sends me all the love and help I need in every moment. I rejoice in all the little details He takes care of for me.

Jesus carries my illness and leads me to new life. All I need to do is be receptive and trust. In dancing, I feel whole again. The Lord delights in my ballet moves and my offering of my trials.

May you too find the peace of Christ in events of your daily life.

Put on your favourite dance music and move to the beat!

40. Is seeking forgiveness your cross?

On a walk in my hometown, away from the bustle of the city, I stepped out of my way to crunch a fallen leaf on the sidewalk. It was very satisfying. Earlier, I had eaten homemade roasted plum jam on peanut butter toast with decaf coffee. The colourful trees in the kitchen window became the backdrop for flying birds. I savoured it, as I did my morning fuel.

Prayer and the sacraments have become fuel for my interior life. If I try to do something on my own steam, I end up exhausted and frustrated. After participating in Mass, I am at peace for the rest of the day.

Sometimes, a day can need more patience, perseverance, and courage than the one before. When I am in a season of illness from bipolar disorder, it is easy to cling to the idols of comfort and fear. I am training my will to choose the good, since my nature is so weak. I don't turn to Jesus enough for anything

I need. It is not always my first option. I can be bitter. My family can't understand what it is like to hear voices or to live on a swing of emotion that can be hard to balance.

The Lord calls us to be like him by carrying our crosses. In the book *Jesus the Way, the Truth, and the Life*, Marcellino D'Ambrosio says Jesus ignores "what usually stops us dead in our tracks—fear of suffering, of ridicule, of abandonment by our friends." People living with a mental illness often feel this way. I know I do.

When I have nightmares, poor sleep, frightening hallucinations, and obsessive intrusive thoughts, I give it all over to Jesus to transform. Often, I picture myself holding on to his neck and burying my head in his shoulders as he carries me to safety.

Thank goodness we don't carry the cross with only our own strength. Jesus takes the weight of our suffering—for he too went through it.

Our cross is lighter when we let go, like the falling leaves, and forgive the people we need to. When we let go, we make more space in our heart for love and compassion for ourselves and our loved ones. It is like making room for new spring flowers. I need to forgive myself as much as others. When I make mistakes or sin, I remind myself that I am loved by God and have compassion for my actions. I make an act of contrition and set a time to go to confession when I can. Jesus wants us to be happy, not glum, about our sinful nature.

Someone said to me the most difficult aspect of living the Our Father prayer is forgiving others. I agree. It takes a lot of effort to give forgiveness to those who have injured us.

I like the formula for forgiveness at the end of confession: "through the ministry of the Church, may God give you pardon and peace. And I absolve you from your sins in the name of the Father, and of the Son and of the Holy Spirit." That feeling of peace I experience helps me to get over the discomfort of baring my soul to Jesus through a priest.

After a recent confession I wanted to sing and dance in thanksgiving. Before I left, the priest said that with the mercy and love God has shown you, show mercy and love to others too.

The freedom received in the sacrament of confession is healing in mind, body and soul. I will keep going back to it.

It takes all kinds of skills along with the sacraments to help me flourish again. Art journaling, walking, and visiting friends help improve my mental health.

The quiet neighbourhood of my family home brings me contentment as I spend time here. Enjoying walks to the pier and through the village, I rediscover the beauty of my small town. More moments of silence and a slower pace is what I needed.

Sometimes carrying our cross looks like finding forgiveness in our hearts. It is a lifelong journey worthy of the peace we desire and need. "He brought me forth into a broad place; he delivered me, because he delighted in me." (Psalm 18:19).

Make some art or visit a friend.

41. Leave "if only" behind

Cold weather is the perfect time to make soup. I pulled out a medium-sized pot and placed it on the stove as I went searching for a few ingredients.

Red lentil soup is one of my favourites. I always top it with a swirl of pepper oil or a dollop of yogurt. This time I added a teaspoon of garam masala for more flavour.

My dad and mom came into the kitchen as the aroma of onions and carrots, caramelizing in a pot, filled the room. When I almost bumped into my dad, he gave me a hug. My mom gave me a squeeze as she took a plate from the cupboard.

The warm kitchen became crowded, but I didn't mind the company. I was at home recuperating, after spending time in the hospital recovering from a recent episode of psychosis and mania.

My brain needs hugs as much as I do. It is sensitive to ongoing stress. New medications were taking time to work and help me find equilibrium again. I kept reminding myself that everything was going to be okay. All things work together for good for those who love God.

When I first got sick and was hospitalized at 17 years old, my family was there for me too. They are like strong trees rooted around me, offering me the care I need. When strong winds come, and they do come, I have learned to bend and sway and lean on the prayers and support of my family.

In my parents' living room, a group of pictures hang on an accent wall. In one there is a cluster of tall trees together, and other paintings show trees on their own. One scene is in a storm, and another a quiet lakeshore. I love this set of paintings. They are powerful reminders of who I have surrounding me. Through all kinds of weather, I have a resilient, caring, and compassionate family.

When I met Margaret Trudeau, after reading her memoir *Changing My Mind*, she asked me a question, "Isn't accepting your illness the hardest part?"

I immediately agreed with her.

That evening she talked about coming to terms with bipolar disorder in her own life. It was a tremendous struggle for her to accept, but her story ended with hope. When I am having a blah kind of day, I remember that it will pass. It's at times like this that I notice grief wanting my attention. I never expected my life to be this way. So many twists and turns. So many uncomfortable side effects to medicine. I grieve, wondering what my life would have been like without mental illness.

I take a deep breath and accept that I have an illness and that's okay. Grieving is a necessary thing to do. I don't want to bury my feelings, and so I find natural and healthy ways to let my emotions out.

I read the lives of the saints, especially St. Therese of Lisieux and St. Josemaria Escriva.

St. Josemaria Escriva writes about the love for the present moment in his homily "Passionately Loving the World."

There he advised, "Leave behind false idealisms, fantasies, and what I usually call 'mystical wishful thinking': If only I hadn't married; if only I had a different job or degree; if only I were in better health; if only I were younger; if only I were older. Instead, turn to the most material and immediate reality, which is where you'll find the Lord."

Finding Jesus in the little moments of the day is the journey I am on. My life turned upside down when I ended up in the hospital, and I had to find peace in the turmoil. If I think about the past, I get depressed and if I think about the future I become anxious. Appreciating the present moment has become my best step forward.

As I heal and care for my mind, body, and soul, I am mindful of how I feel throughout the day. Grief sometimes shows up too. A bowl of hot homemade soup feeds the body well. Family and friends bring necessary companionship. With Jesus' love and protection, I can handle anything.

Make a pot of your favourite soup.

42. Is connection on your "have a good day" checklist?

The connections I make, with friends and family, lifted my spirits as I recovered.

Antonio Neves, speaker and author of *Stop Living on Autopilot,* has a checklist of five things he needs to do every day to have a good day. One of those things is connection.

Connection is my most important way to turn a bad day into a great one. Making plans with friends helps my mental health.

On a beautiful early December day, my friend from the hospital and I met for brunch. We related to each other's frustrations, wins, and hopes and dreams over eggs Benny. Later, we walked along the seawall. Seagulls called, the sun shone through the clouds, and wind whipped our hair.

I'm blessed to have a pen pal, Treasa, in Dublin who sends me letters and frequent email messages. Two years ago, she read an article about my journey with bipolar disorder and faith online.

While I was recuperating, she sent me a birthday gift in the mail: a package of makeup, a Miraculous Medal, and a beautiful emerald rosary. It boosted my mood, as I was feeling desolate because I couldn't do many things at the time. I was trying to be patient and take it easy.

I was not supposed to put too much pressure on producing anything.

Treasa happens to be the same age as me and is kind and thoughtful. We exchange cards in the mail and almost daily messages. We share our daily goings-on and our prayer intentions.

When I was sick in the hospital, she told me she visited her church and prayed in front of the Blessed Sacrament for me to get better. It helped me feel like I would be okay.

The connections I have made from being vulnerable and sharing my story have improved my life. I have made many new friends who can relate and are inspiring, resilient individuals.

Human connection can heal a broken heart or a struggling mind. I am blessed with many deep and meaningful friendships.

While staying with my parents in their small town, I felt isolated but connected at the same time. Thanks to coffee dates, email, and social media I am close to the relationships that mean the most to me. Our stories continue to weave in and out of each other's lives.

My life's tapestry is a multi-faceted creative pursuit of love. When I am snug by the fireplace reading a food memoir, I am content knowing I am loved. My Saviour, family, and friends show me that I am the beloved.

Without love, I would wither and not be able to recover. When I get anxious as I am about to fall asleep, I give all my worries to Jesus. The anxiety fills my head, and I have difficulty breathing. Asking Jesus to take care of everything helps as I remind myself to breathe deeply. I imagine the Lord holding me in His arms, which seems to help.

I wait for all the uncomfortable symptoms to pass. I'm most connected to Jesus at Mass, in the Eucharist, or talking to Him in my heart. I am nourished by His body and feel His presence.

Treasa and I may be long-distance friends, but she sees me and checks in with me. It warms my heart.

After I left the residential short-term emergency stay, I stayed in contact with two women who were companions for me there. Our breakfast, lunch, and dinnertime chats were my favourite parts of the day. We would talk about what we were going to do when we were released.

We had rooms side by side, which was handy when we were self-isolating due to a COVID outbreak. We all tested negative but had to stay in our small bedrooms for five days. We sent each other songs and encouraging messages, and I would sing for them. They could hear the worship and love songs through their walls and said, "Keep it up!"

Connection to my friends helps fill the ache inside for love and belonging. Only God can truly fill this big ache. His gifts of relationship with his Son and the relationships we have lift us up and strengthen us. When we see His gifts of connection, we can hold on to hope.

Reach out to a friend.

43. When it feels like He's not there

You are loved.

You matter.

Don't give up.

Don't be afraid.

These words heal and have brought me comfort many times. I need to hear these words now as much as I did when I was in the hospital.

I believed the lie that I could do everything by my own effort alone.

I was doing everything in my power to juggle projects and relationships.

God said, "Let me help."

No, I got this.

I burned out and was overcome with psychosis and mania. Though it's not all my fault: sometimes things just break down, especially with chronic mental illness. My brain is a marvelous and complex organ. The medicine wasn't providing enough support for me to have balance.

In the emergency waiting room I trembled and fell to the floor shouting, "I can't do this alone anymore!"

Later I prayed to Jesus, *I can't do this. I am giving you all my projects, plans and problems. I'm stepping back. Jesus, you have the relief I need. I don't have the answers. I can't do life on my own. I need you, Jesus!*

Two nurses helped my mom lift me off the floor into a wheelchair to take me to a calmer room. They looked me in the eyes and said, "Lisa, you're going to be okay."

They held my hands and shoulders as my whole body shook violently. I changed into a hospital gown and lay on a mattress on the floor in a small dark room. I was scared, trembling, and hoping for peace.

One of the nurses who took my pulse was very kind. I asked her if she had seen the *Chosen* series, because I felt a bit like Mary Magdalene from the first episode, although my experience was very different. When the emergency doctor came in to check my vital signs, I asked him if this feeling was what jumping out of an airplane feels like.

never jumped out of an airplane."

Even though I didn't feel Jesus' presence at that moment, looking back I know He was with me in the hospital. He was with me and my mom as we checked in. He was at my side when they brought me upstairs to give me a room. And He has never left. As Father Fernando Ocariz, prelate of Opus Dei, said in his Christmas message, "God is looking at us lovingly at every moment. Realizing we are constantly accompanied by God's love" (Fr. Fernando Ocariz's Christmas Greeting 2021 via video).

Yet I still can feel abandoned, and that is when I need to hear those healing words.

You are loved.

You matter.

Don't give up.

Don't be afraid.

That is when my confidence in His love for me is tested.

When things are going well, I believe—without a doubt—in his love and kindness. It's in times of darkness and trial that I am tested and find it difficult to hold on to hope.

My life will unfold in unknown ways, and I want to trust God through it. He cares for me and you with His very own life. He came to us as a baby at Christmas and promises to give us lives of joy. I hold onto the belief that good things are coming. That the best is not behind but ahead.

Hope doesn't mean that you have a smile on your face all day. It is the quiet certitude that God, who created the heavens and earth, sent His son and will take care of our needs.

My experience in the hospital is proof of healing. I came out with increased self-compassion, tenderness, and love.

I am working on changing negative thoughts into positive thinking. I am taking the medicine prescribed. I am doing therapy. I am attending Mass and confession. All these things help my body, mind, and soul heal.

I am letting God help me with my plans and goals. *I won't give up. I believe.*

"For God alone my soul waits in silence, for my hope is from him. He only is my rock and my salvation, my fortress; I shall not be shaken" (Psalms 62:5-6).

Check out the Chosen series.

44. Holiness is a lifelong journey

Holiness—is it possible for someone with a mental illness? To devote one's life to do the will of God. To sanctify one's work and family life.

It's a possibility and a work of grace for all of us. We can't make ourselves holy on our own. Allowing the Holy Spirit to move in our minds and hearts, and to act in good will, helps us get to heaven.

I've been reflecting on holiness and how my personal sin affects the community. After a recent confession, I realized I could fall more in love with Jesus. I would want to sin less when I had my eyes on him.

We need perseverance because we are weak and fall repeatedly.

Jesus loves us so wildly. I can't even imagine how much he loves me! His love is immense and as hard to fathom as the size of the universe, which contains countless stars larger than the sun.

Arise Shine & Live

Talking on the phone with a friend about the struggles and silver linings of mental illness, I shared my own experiences and we discussed those of our families. We switched topics and encouraged each other as we strive for holiness in our lives. I paced my room in excited passion. We swapped quotes from Scripture and recent homilies we had heard.

The conversation with my friend warmed my heart and reminded me that I'm not alone in this adventurous journey of faith.

My favourite stories about long journeys are C. S. Lewis's Chronicles of Narnia series and J.R.R Tolkien's *The Lord of the Rings*. When the Pevensie children meet Aslan for the first time in Narnia, it's thrilling. And when Frodo the hobbit agrees to go on a treacherous journey to save Middle Earth, it inspires me.

I also enjoyed *Letters to Myself from the End of the World* on WILDGOOSE.TV. It is a series of conversations between Father Dave Pivonka and Emily Stimpson Chapman based on the chapters of her book with the same title. I love the authentic and casual conversations they have filmed in her home.

Before watching the videos I was in a dry, desert-like state, but during them I wanted to draw closer to Jesus in prayer. Prompted by the Holy Spirit after watching one video, I called up my friend and we prayed a Rosary together. I'm so glad we did: we had many intentions to pray for and the company was a spiritual boost for the soul.

With my phone tucked in the folds of my blankets, I sat in bed holding my blue-beaded rosary. My friend led a Scriptural reflection on each mystery of the Rosary as we prayed. Her smooth voice floated softly from my cell phone speaker and brought me peace. My anxiety often catches up with me at night, and that evening Rosary over the phone helped me to stay calm.

It's a blessing to have friends who I can call any time for a chat or a prayer. With chronic illness, prayer is a soothing balm. When I don't feel like praying, I can find inspiration in someone else who does—whether it's with friends or family, or with a popular app that contains an amazing amount of Catholic content, Hallow.

I used Hallow in the hospital last fall when I couldn't sleep. I could hear trains blasting their horns at all hours of the night and early in the morning. Nurses would open the door and flash a light on me to see if I was sleeping. It wasn't restful, so I would pray the Divine Mercy Chaplet and Rosary on Hallow. I listened to the soothing voices of Jonathan Roumie (Jesus from *The Chosen* series) and Bishop Barron as they prayed.

I'm so happy that Jesus provides me with the people, places, and tools I need to nurture my interior life. They all help me on the lifelong journey of holiness—a path to sanctity.

We are all invited to become saints, and in the hospital, I could feel all the prayers of my family and friends. They held me up and encouraged me to keep hoping for a swift recovery.

I pray I can craft a life of holiness—by picking up the cross of bipolar disorder, living a life of faith, and depending on God.

Find a book to encourage you whether it be an old classic or something new.

45. A fresh perspective

One cloudy January day, my brother and I went for a walk in the forest. The tall trees hid the sky. Moss covered branches reached over the path. We moved briskly along the trail.

Dog walkers and joggers passed us as we hiked around the park. We saw a juvenile eagle perched on a branch above our heads. The steady beat of our steps and the moist air refreshed my tired muscles.

Not a single anxious thought went through my head while we were in the forest. I was present in the moment. The sounds and smells of the clear brook and evergreen trees awakened my senses and brought back memories of camping trips as a young girl with my family.

I have enjoyed being in nature since I rode in the backpack on my dad's shoulders in the woods. I remember going to Golden Ears Park. My younger sister and I pretended pine cones were dolls.

Collecting rocks and shells was part of the fun on a beach visit.

I picked up a pink and orange rock that was smooth. Such beautiful stones filled the path. Each one a different shape and colour. My brother led the way down the trail. I was filled with wonder as I walked the winding route through trees and creek beds. A meditative walk.

I have started praying lectio divina, to listen more to God speaking into my life. I open my Bible and read a passage from the gospels, a psalm, or a letter. I pray for an openness to hear God's voice through the words I am reading. I read one passage three times. I pick one word that stands out from the first reading. Then a second one, and the last reading I choose a phrase that is speaking to me.

This practice has nourished my soul. The words echo for me throughout the next day, giving me a feeling of safety and security. Recently from Isaiah 49:8-13 the words "establish," and "heritage," spoke powerfully to me. So did the phrase, "in a time of favour I have answered you." These words brought comfort as I had been worrying about my future.

The Lord has always provided for me. Reading the Bible, I can hear God's voice. Words have power. Scripture is the living word.

Like the sounds and smells of the forest, God's words bring fresh perspective and awaken my heart. They help me to slow down and give space to hear the call of being a disciple.

Often I fill my mind and ears with too much music, podcasts, and other media, which can block God's voice. I begin to falter in my prayer life and lose sight of my loving friendship with Jesus.

Every day is a chance to begin again. To bring Jesus into the centre of my life, and ask Him to be my Lord and Saviour. Though faith is a gift, I pray that I will always love the Lord and will return to him.

In Emily Stimpson Chapman's book *Letters to Myself from the End of the World*, she says, "But you don't need God someday. You need Him today. You need to talk to Him now and listen to Him now and call upon Him now in the midst of your crazy, chaotic, spit-up-laden life."

Maintaining my mental health sometimes seems like I am fighting a crazy, chaotic war. Yet, the Lord is amidst the suffering. He is there in the anxious thoughts and sleepless nights. He heals me from mania and psychosis. God is good.

When we arrived at a brook, my brother and I stopped and marvelled at the peacefulness of the running

Arise Shine &

water over the rocks. To remember it later, I capt a short video.

God's grace often works through people, such as the walk in the forest with my brother Adrian did. My cousin Sarah gifted me a book by Aimee Chase called *Present not Perfect: A Journal for Slowing Down, Letting Go and Loving Who You Are*, which reminded me to find the beauty in the moment and not be a perfectionist. Whether it's pausing to smell the fresh evergreen trees or admiring an eagle, it helps me to embrace my "wonderfully imperfect life."

Pay attention to sights and smells that bring you refreshment.

46. A chef's healing cooking

As I walked along rain-soaked farm fields, getting my daily exercise, I asked myself, "What truly feeds us?"

Doughnuts from a local boutique donut shop delight but don't nourish. The Eucharist both delights and nourishes me. I get excited when it is time for communion, even though I don't feel the same intensity at every Mass.

The Eucharist has become even more precious to me because of the obstacles of COVID-19.

Attending Mass in person is the highlight of my Sunday. Attending daily mass during the week, when I can, makes me happy as well.

The Eucharist helps me find my way through the darkness. I've experienced many uncomfortable and difficult things in the hospital and while changing to new medications. There are side effects, and they take getting used to.

Arise Shine & Live

The sacred body of Christ, my beloved, has become the ultimate comfort food. I mean this with the utmost respect. Jesus' presence in the holy host nourishes me in a way that no other food can.

When my family has breakfast with bacon, eggs, and pancakes, it gives us time to bond. My brothers and sisters make each other laugh. We talk about troubling circumstances and stressful situations in the world. We have each other's back when needed and support one another with a myriad of gifts. We are all unique—makers, writers, singers, musicians, innovators, and peacekeepers.

Anthony, the kind and talented chef at the residence where I stayed during my recovery, served up plates of tasty food and also smiles and encouragement. At one point, I was the only patient after all the others were discharged. He made the most flavourful thanksgiving dinner for me and the people next door. I had never eaten turkey that tender.

It was a time for being fed, a time to restore the senses. My soul is touched through the senses.

Anthony cooked pasta, spicy nachos, and homemade hamburgers. Chow mein, perogies, and roasts. So many comfort foods, like macaroni and cheese, pizza, and soups.

When I was in self-isolation due to a COVID outbreak in the residence, I couldn't swallow food because of my anxiety. Shakes and sandwiches cut up into small bite size pieces were sent to me. Anthony always spoke to me with the kindness and empathy of a good friend.

I wrote a poem inspired by his cooking.

My Prayer is Food

Garlic green beans with scallions
Creamy mashed potatoes
Peppercorn and rosemary pork roast
Brought dinner time healing
From my head to my toes

Fuel for my body
Reminds me of the Lord's supper
Food for the body
Prayer for the soul

My duty and delight
To plant, to grow
To prepare, to cook
To eat
Each day and night.

I am grateful to Anthony and his part in improving my health and wellbeing. For me, his cooking was as important as the care of the nurses, mental health workers, and psychiatrists. I remember the smell of spicy chicken wafting towards me from the barbeque on a cloudy day. Everyone has a gift to serve others. He found his.

Even during difficult times, Christ never changes. Through it all Jesus remains available to us in the Eucharist anywhere in the world, every day.

St. John Paul II said, "The Eucharistic Sacrifice is the 'source and summit of all Christian Life.' It is a single Sacrifice that embraces everything. It is the greatest treasure of the Church. It is her life."

Now that feeds me. Thanks be to God for every blessing He sends, opportunity for Mass, family bonds, and Chef Anthony.

Plan a dinner party with friends or family.

47. Inspired by an Italian pianist and composer

I don't know if it's the cold, fog, and rain that have permeated my interior landscape, or feeling stuck in a pandemic. Whenever I get into a funk, I look for inspiration: music, a quote from a saint, or a new colourful shirt. But where I need to look for inspiration is to Jesus.

Listening to stories of other people who have come through a trial when I'm stuck gives me hope.

Alberto Giurioli, an Italian pianist and composer, and I connected on Instagram. He shared his neoclassical music on many platforms. I liked the first few songs I listened to, "Following Yourself" and "Tutto è bellissimo."

I said to him in a direct message, "I'm editing my column to your piano music." He replied, "Cool, glad you like what I do."

Alberto is a mental health warrior too. He fought to stay here when it got tough. He started playing piano when he was a boy. At one point he wanted to give up when he was bored and his hands hurt from playing a grand piano. His parents encouraged him to continue, and that is when he began to like it.

While in London pursuing his dream, a video of Alberto playing a street piano went viral and kicked-off his career. Since then, he has played in many sold-out theatres and has millions of downloads.

It is a struggle to feel the gift of life when depressed or despairing. Though I was not depressed, I was tired of winter and so many public health restraints because of COVID. I prayed for the end of the pandemic and the return of more social interactions.

While reading Scripture, the words from Matthew 8:7 jumped off the page for me. "I will come and cure him." Oh, how I would love to receive a cure for my mental illness. Jesus doesn't want us to suffer. He wants us to be free of disease, addiction, and sin. I am learning to hope with greater spirit in His power to heal. I imagine what it would be like for Him to heal me too. Especially when reading about the miracles He performed in the Gospels.

It is not impossible. It's something that I never thought to ask for until a few friends asked if I would like to receive prayers for physical healing.

My mind needs restoration. Healing for healthy neurotransmitters and rewiring of fear-based pathways.

My first response is to doubt that Jesus would ever do something this grand for me. I know someone who lives without the problems of bipolar disorder, even though she has a diagnosis. What faith I would need to have to ask the Lord for what He desires for me!

God is good and won't let me down. Healing can take time. It's amazing how I have everything I need in the moment from Him. I am never left without His love.

The gift of being alive is an act of His love. He loves us, and we exist in that love.

It was a pleasure to find Alberto's music. He offers his talent to add beauty to the lives of others. Seeing how he uses his gift for the world inspires me.

When I'm bored, uninspired, or lacking peace, I ask myself if Jesus is in the centre. Have I been putting Him first? Or am I disappointed with the distractions of my own making?

"He will come in His own time, and when you least expect it. Hope in Him more than ever" (Myra).

Trusting God through the long haul even when your path forward is not clear is hard to do. I don't know if I will be cured of my mental illness or if it will be a lifelong challenge. I don't know how long the pandemic will go on. I do know that winter will end and spring will come.

I look forward to spending more time with Jesus during Lent to believe in His healing love and to listening to beautiful music from talented artists.

Say a prayer of trust to the Lord and ask for healing in your life.

48. God delights in you through all your troubles

One sunny Saturday a friend and I walked through a park by a river, chatting about her work as a teacher. The trees were still bare, so our view of the river was unobstructed. The air was cool but not too cold. I sipped a hot drink as we talked. Andrea mentioned what she said to her student who felt the need to fit in.

"It's okay to be different. Everyone has strengths and weaknesses. Everyone learns in different ways, and that's okay. The important thing is that you understand how you learn and what works for you and embrace it."

Her words reminded me that you do not need to fit in to be worthy.

She also said, "We often tend to conform and be like everyone else. We forget to acknowledge our own beauty, strengths, and talents."

Sometimes I feel unworthy because I have bipolar disorder. I wonder what it would be like without this diagnosis. Would I have compassion for others struggling with anxiety, depression, bipolar disorder, eating disorders, schizophrenia, and other invisible illnesses?

Or would I have missed the opportunity to meet them in hospital wards and support groups? Their presence helps me realize I'm not alone. I'm not strange. That it's okay to have differences.

"What I thought was my end was only Your beginning," declares Sean Feucht in his song "You delight in me."

I learned so much from the kindness of the other patients in the hospital last September. Some brought me extra orange juice, gave me the best colouring pages, and kept me company.

Being locked in a ward with strangers was not always comfortable. Yet they were some of the kindest people.

Some cracked jokes to make me smile, and one taught me how to play a magic trick with cards. A few raced along beside me on the stationary bikes as we exercised. Some picked out their favourite movies to share with me.

One held my hand and twirled me around the room as I danced ballet. Some played ping-pong with me and gave me great competition.

One made drawings for me to take home. One taught me about football as I watched along with him.

All of this made me feel delighted in. These patients were going through all kinds of trauma and trouble. They were thoughtful, supportive, and loving.

The nurses and doctor were also very caring. I could ask them for anything I needed. They didn't seem frustrated when asked for a phone charger or a movie, even if they were busy. They made us popcorn and tea.

Sometimes, the behaviour of upset patients scared me. Their tempers made me want to hide. I felt homesick.

My parents were so good at coming to drop off items I needed. Because of COVID, I couldn't have visitors, so I waved to them through the bars of the fifth-floor window. We blew kisses to each other. My family is a huge support to me. I am so blessed and feel their delight in me, even when things get difficult.

I also had the privilege of speaking to three priests during my stay: a friend, a spiritual director, and a professional in psychology. My phone was a way to connect with the outside world. And, oh, how I needed to!

Thinking it over, I wouldn't change my life with an illness, although receiving healing and a cure would be amazing. I do notice transformations in my life through prayer and the sacraments.

God delights in me. And God delights in you.

You are a beloved child of God. It's okay to be different. It's a beautiful thing to be unique.

Whatever ails you can bring you closer to the heart of the Father. I continue to bring all my afflictions to God, and He showers me with affection. His love is there for me every day. No matter what I do, how I am feeling. It never changes.

His love is indescribable. I am especially reminded of His love when I go to Mass and receive the Eucharist.

"I know I captured all your affection. That's the end of the story. You've always been for me," Feucht sings.

Listen to "You delight in Me" by Sean Feucht.

49. Even in adversity there can be joy

My friend from the hospital moved to Vancouver Island. No more hikes and outings together unless one of us takes a ferry ride. When we hiked in Minnekhada park, I could see her love of nature, and I appreciated her patience with my slower pace. I worried about not being able to get together as often once she moved.

The Lord is patient with me too. Every time I turn away from Him, He invites me back. He loves me at both my best and my worst.

Our last visit was a walk along the seawall on an afternoon promising rain. I felt excitement for her new chapter and, at the same time, it was bittersweet. I would miss our long walks and chats. We reminisced about our shared experiences in the hospital. We talked about the therapy that helped and the hobbies we had taken up or put down.

"Even in adversity there can be joy in the assurance that the Divine Master Himself died through the cross as the condition of His Resurrection. Joy can be felt in both prosperity and adversity," wrote Archbishop Fulton Sheen in *Way to Happiness*.

Some days I struggle with anxiety more than others, which takes a physical and emotional toll.

I am resilient. I know when to take a cooling off period or to keep going. Comfort isn't guaranteed. "Only God is guaranteed," as Peter Kreeft writes in *Heaven, the Heart's Deepest Longing*.

I need the mindset of Christ. The resurrection attitude. No one comes to the Father except through Him. There is no way I can do anything on my own steam. I don't want to have a self-help kind of faith; I want a deep trust in the Lord's provision. I seek to do what God is calling me to do in my work, play, rest, and relationships. I make plans, and I am willing to change them when the Lord shows me another way.

In adoration one morning, my stomach growled like a tiger, which fed into my prayer. *I am so hungry and poor, Lord. I need your love to fill me up. Please take care of all Your people and the dear ones close to me. Lord, I will always hunger for heaven. I want to take the road to heaven. Lead me. Show me what it's like to be fully alive. Transform my pain from the past year into something beautiful.*

The Lord always supports us. Recently I moved back to the city, and I felt completely provided for by Him in all the details of the move. Jesus gave His all using every muscle in His body to carry the cross and to give up His life for us.

My response is gratitude and joy. Especially because He broke the chains of sin for us. His resurrection is the power of God. How can I not be joyful?

I know that there are great things in store for my friend who is moving to the Island. Sometimes, there are seasons for friendships and sometimes friendships last a lifetime. We walked a path of pain together, although we have different mental health struggles and paths of healing. I found healing in her companionship.

Jesus was not a stranger to pain and anguish. Betrayed, He suffered and died. Mental illness can weigh heavy on the person who suffers and on those who love and support that person.

Finding a support group or therapy, or someone to talk to can be helpful. "There is only one cure for fear—trust in God," wrote Caryll Houselander in *The Reed of God*. "If we fear for ourselves or if we fear for others, it is all the same: trust in God is the only remedy."

Spring, along with the promise of Easter joy, brings me a freshness in my heart and soul. Jesus' new life assures me that I can trust in him. I have risen from the pain of the past year and found a new chapter to write.

In the early mornings, as I prepare for the day, I am grateful for another one. My days are numbered, and I don't know when it will be my time to go. Knowing that this life on earth is passing and that heaven is eternal, I live with my heart open to the Lord. I offer my weaknesses and my talents, hoping He can make me into a holy woman.

Jesus has won the victory over death and over generations of mental illness. I continue to pray for healing for my family and the families of the world. Without His sacrifice we couldn't know this joy of salvation. I believe in miracles, and I hope to see them in the lives of my family, friends, and colleagues.

Think of something you are grateful for and write it in a journal.

50. The bravest thing you can do is ask for help

Pick up the pen and be brave.

Five years ago, these words came into my heart during prayer. The Lord asked me to let go of the stigma and shame of having a mental illness.

I had been carrying it around for so long, and it was time to surrender and to write about it.

I clung to the safety of anonymity and the invisibility of the label—bipolar disorder—that I lived with. I was hiding in my pain. I thought everyone who knew me would think mental illness was a weakness, not a sickness. My fears of people finding out reared in my head like ugly cartoon monsters. For a long time, I trusted only a few people with my story.

When I opened up to friends and told my story, they didn't run away and I knew I was not alone. For years, my self-identity was centred around having a disability. I began to see that I am not my illness.

I have an illness. Language is important to live the truth of who you are.

I am a beloved daughter of God.

This realization frees me from the monsters of shame, fear, and anger and allows me to live in abundance.

On a recent workday, I went for a walk to recharge. I brought a picnic lunch and settled at a wooden table in the garden outside of the Healthy Minds Centre. As I sat down, I noticed faint green writing in front of me. Written on the table were the words, "It's okay to not be okay. It's okay, healing takes time."

I smiled. That note was what I needed at that moment. I was tense and stressed and worried. The message jumped out at me even though the words were faded from the sun and rain.

I read once that "Asking for help is one of the bravest things we'll ever do" (Brené Brown). It takes humility to reach out. I turn to family and friends when I am lonely, afraid, or unable to cope. "Don't you think the things people are most ashamed of are the things they can't help?" wrote C.S. Lewis in *Till We Have Faces*.

When I spend time in prayer with Jesus, I'm made aware of my wholeness. The Lord is the ultimate physician. "It is the Lord ... who heals all your diseases, who redeems your life from the pit, who crowns you with steadfast love and mercy" (Psalms 103: 3-4).

He gives medicine and psychiatrists, counsellors and therapists, to bring us healing. We can't do life alone. God, who is a communion of persons, made us to need each other.

So, I began to write, and write, and write. I started to journal and wrote poems and short prose. I worked on writing a couple of books (which are still unpublished works). I began to write for *The B.C. Catholic* following the encouragement of friends and the movement of the Holy Spirit. I delight in writing. Discovering the joy of writing and being vulnerable brings me such comfort and connection. As my favourite high school English teacher would say, "It's cathartic."

My journals keep filling up. I keep Post-it notes and loose papers with ideas, musings, and quotes. My room is full of books – a small library. My reading list is always long. I spend many evenings curled up with a cup of tea and a good book. I am always looking to improve my writing skills. I am learning from great writers like Austen, Lewis, and Tolkien.

Finding my identity in Christ, my life has become a beautiful unfolding tale. Reflecting on it provides me with hope because the Lord has gifted me with good things and people. I am grateful for the unveiling of who I am; I look forward to who I will become. I no longer wear masks to hide the fact that I have bipolar disorder.

I'm unashamed and do not carry stigma from having a mental illness. I like the lyrics from the country song *I Got a Truck* by Devin Dawson, who sings "'Cause I got a song, I got a story to tell, I got a reason for living."

And then, "I got a dream and a hope and a prayer ... I got the drive and the grit and the spirit."

We all have a story to share. There is room for all our stories. And we can be brave in sharing them because our hope is in the Lord.

Do you feel you can write or tell someone your story?

Acknowledgements

To my dear family to whom I owe my gratitude for support in my illness and recovery. I love you all so much!

To my faithful Mom, who believed that my life was not over when I became sick and continues to support and love me through all the ups and downs.

To my dearest Dad, thank you for your bear hugs and listening to me read every column before I published it.

To Daniel, my eldest brother, thank you for your friendship with movie nights and dinners and for smiling when I make silly jokes.

To Adrian, thank you for sitting in the psychiatrist's waiting room with a cup of coffee for me during many years of my recovery.

To Monica, thank you for being my best friend who is always up for an adventure.

To Julia, thank you for dropping everything to be with me countless times when I needed company.

To Thomas, my youngest brother, thank you for your encouragement for my work.

To my friends, who have given me inspiration and encouragement and believe that my storytelling can encourage others to live with joy, thank you. Especially: Stephanie G., Sarah, Anna, Eliza, Rose, Agnieszka, Alana, Aggie, Amber C., Jazz, Talia, Trisha, Priscilla, Melgie, Mary-Jane, Stephanie D., Rachel, Winetta, Jamie, Megan, Gemma, Andrea, Stephanie G.C., Allixe, Desiree, Evan, David, Christine, Liz, Dia, Vida, Angelica, Alexandra, April, Krystal, Merve, Jemma, Michelle, Marie-Elena, Krissy, Kathy, Rob, Pat G., Michel, Sandy, Lesya, Kleah, Jennifer, Nicole, Inca, Paul, Alan Y., Makani, Lisa M., Leah, Gina, Michael, Darren.

To Madonna House Vancouver, thank you for bringing me communion in the hospital and for giving me a place to write and pray.

Previous versions of these essays appeared in *The B.C. Catholic* from 2018-2022. My gratitude to the editors, especially Paul Schratz.

To my editor Angela Kublik, thank you for tireless work and encouragement.

I would like to thank all the health professionals, counsellors, psychiatrists, psychologists, occupational support workers, nurses who have walked beside me on my journey and continue to do so. Thank you all for your loving support, wisdom, and guidance.

Works Cited

All biblical quotes are from:

The Holy Bible: Revised Standard Version Second Catholic Edition. Ignatius Press, 2001.

1. **Anxiety with my groceries**

   Low. Abraham. *The Wisdom of Doctor Low: Words to Live By.* Recovery Inc., 2019.

3. **Praise and lament**

   Swinton Jon. "Interpersonal Relationships and Mental Health." Redefining Healing Seminars. Tenth Church, Vancouver. 15 May 2019.

4. **Finding purpose out of darkness**

   Heller, Cat, host. "How I got here." *Cathy Heller Presents Don't Keep Your Day Job*, episode 94, Authentic, 25 November 2019, https://www.dontkeepyourdayjob.com/episodes/how-i-got-here.

Rumpel, Lisa. *The Resilient Catholic.* https://resilientcatholic.home.blog/.

The Sanctuary Course for Catholics. The Sanctuary Mental Health Ministries, 2020, https://sanctuarymentalhealth.org/catholics/.

5. **It takes a forest to lift a spirit**

Wohllenben, Peter. *The Hidden Life of Trees.* Greystone Books, 2015, pp. 8, 12.

8. **Whether your song is happy or sad, God is listening**

Colbert, Stephen. "Overcoming grief and loss as a child." Interview by Anderson Cooper. CNN Interview, 16 August 2019, https://www.cnn.com/videos/us/2019/08/16/colbert-ac360-intv-grief-loss-father-brothers-god-religion-bts-vpx.cnn. Accessed 27 November 2022.

Personal Projects Course. Pacific Institute of Family Education, Vancouver, 2018.

9. **Jesus' resurrection fuels my joy**

Pope Francis. "Homily of his Holiness Pope Francis." *Easter Vigil in the Holy Night of Easter.* Vatican Basilica, 20 April 2019, https://www.vatican.va/content/francesco/en/homilies/2019/documents/papa-francesco_20190420_omelia-vegliapasquale.html.

Raffi. "All I Really Need." *Raffi on Broadway: A Family Concert*, Universal Music Canada, 1993. CD.

Saint Pope John Paul II. "Angelus." *Apostolic Journey to the Far East and Oceania*. Adelaide, Australia, 30 November 1986. https://www.vatican.va/content/john-paul-ii/en/angelus/1986/documents/hf_jp-ii_ang_19861130.html.

10. We need the support of others

Fraser, Henry [@henryfraser0]. "Disabled people need to see themselves in others. We need to see others like us achieving, living and inspiring." *Twitter*, Jul. 28, 2019, https://twitter.com/henryfraser0/status/1155491058878418944.

12. Never give up on hope

Alar, Father Chris. *Divine Mercy After Suicide*. Marian Fathers of the Immaculate Conception of the B.V.M., 2019.

Kowalska, St. Maria Faustina. *Diary of Saint Maria Faustina Kowalska: Divine Mercy in My Soul.* Marian Press, 2005.

Pope John Paul II. *Pope John Paul II: In My Own Words.* Compiled by Anthony F. Chiffolo, Gramercy Books, 2022.

US Catholic Church. *Catechism of the Catholic Church.* Doubleday, 1995

14. Quebec churches cured my cold and loneliness

Pope Benedict XVI. *Encyclical Letter Pec Salvi of the Supreme Pontif Benedict XVI to the Bishops, Priests and Deacons, Men and Women Religious and all the Lay Faithful on Christian Hope*, sec. 33, 30 November 2007. https://www.vatican.va/content/benedict-xvi/en/encyclicals/documents/hf_ben-xvi_enc_20071130_spe-salvi.html

16. Stand by me, Lord

King, Ben E. "Stand By Me." *Don't Play That Song (You Lied)*, Atlantic Records, 1962. CD.

17. God wants us to be happy

St. John XXIII. "The Daily Decalogue of Pope John XXIII." Qtd by Tarcisio Bertone,

Eucharistic Concelebration Commemorating Pope John XXIII on his Memorial. 11 October 2006. https://www.vatican.va/roman_curia/secretariat_state/card-bertone/2006/documents/rc_seg-st_20061011_john-xxiii_en.html

18. Seasons of blues, seasons of beauty

Fyodor Dostoevsky. *The Idiot.* Vintage Classics, 2012, pp. 383.

19. Who are your Jedi?

Star Wars: The Rise of Skywalker. Directed by J. J. Abrams, Lucas Film/Bad Robot Productions, 2019.

20. Collect your blessings

Santos, Laurie. *Psychology and the Good Life*, Yale University, 2020, https://www.coursera.org/.

21. Home is where God is

Downs, Annie F. *100 Days to Brave: Devotions for Unlocking Your Most Courageous Self*, Zondervan, 2017, pp. 216.

22. Resilience and resurrection in a pandemic

Greitens, Eric. *Resilience: Hard-won Wisdom for Living a Better Life*, HarperCollins, 2015.

Miller, Archbishop Michael. "Easter message." Holy Rosary Cathedral, Vancouver, April 12, 2020.

24. "Just to be alive is a grand thing"

Christie, Agatha. *Agatha Christie, An Autobiography*, Dodd Mead, 1977.

26. The prayer in doing chores

Harter, Michael. *Hearts on Fire: Praying with Jesuits*, Loyola Press, 2004, pp. 102-103.

27. Gifts and crosses

Kruse, Talia. "Blog entry," *Mental Health for Holiness*. Accessed 2017. https://www.mentalhealthforholiness.com/

Pope John Paul I. "General Audience." Wednesday, 20 September 1978. 20 September 1978. https://www.vatican.va/content/john-paul-i/en/audiences/documents/hf_jp-i_aud_20091978.html.

28. **When life goes up in smoke, keep a sense of humour, kindness, and grit**

    Fernandez, Francis. *In Conversations with God*, Vol. 5, Scepter,1989.

29. **Prayer of a "silly woman in front of the tabernacle"**

    Berry, Wendell. *Farming: A Hand Book*. Catapult, 2011.

    Low, Abraham. *Mental Health Through Will Training*, Willet, 1997.

30. **Redesign your living space and unclutter your mind for Jesus**

    Design Doctors. Indigenius, 2018. *Amazon Prime*, primevideo.com.

    Houselander, Caryll. *The Reed of God*, Ave Maria Press, 2006.

    "CCO's Apostle's Prayer." *Catholic Christian Outreach*. https://cco.ca/evangelization-prayers/#:~:text=Holy%20Spirit%20I%20welcome%20you,inside%20the%20city%20of%20man.

31. **When your heart dips low, turn to Jesus**

    Keller, Helen. *The Open Door*, Doubleday, 1957.

32. Riches are in relationships

Harvey, Jane Trufant. *Ask Him, Simple Words to Jumpstart Your Conversation with God*, Wellspring, 2020, pp.150.

Merton, Thomas. *Love and Living*. Edited by Naomi Burton Stone and Patrick Hart, Mariner Books, 1985, pp. 27.

34. Making use of therapy, sleep, and a good dose of laughter

Williams, Robins. Quoted by Amy Finn. "90 Robin Williams Quotes on Life, Love, and Happiness." *Quote Ambition*, https://www.quoteambition.com/robin-williams-quotes/.

Pope Paul VI. "Guadete In Domino." *Apostolic Exhortation of His Holiness Paul VI on Christian Joy*, 9 May 1975, https://www.vatican.va/content/paul-vi/en/apost_exhortations/documents/hf_p-vi_exh_19750509_gaudete-in-domino.html.

35. You're not a robot

Bottaro, Gregory. *The Mindful Catholic: Finding God One Moment at a Time*, Wellspring, 2018.

Our Mission, Our Vision. Catholic Independent Schools of Vancouver Archdiocese, July 2022, https://cisva.bc.ca/info/mission-statement/.

Farber, Steve. *The Radical Edge: Another Personal Lesson in Extreme Leadership*, Bard Press, 2014.

Kowalska, Saint Maria Faustina. *Diary of Saint Maria Faustina Kowalska: Divine Mercy in My Soul*, Marian Press, 2004.

Low, Abraham. *Mental Health Through Will Training*, Willet, 1997.

36. All shall be well

Julian of Norwich. *Showings*, Paulist Press, 1978.

Jacoby, Sarah. *Can I Sit with You?* Chronicle Books, 2021.

37. Choose an attitude of hope

Frankl, Victor. *Man's Search for Meaning*, Beacon Press, 2006.

38. Writing as a form of prayer and healing

Clarkson, Sarah. *Book Girl: A Journey through the Treasures and Transforming Power of a Reading Life*, Tyndale House Publishers, 2018.

40. Is seeking forgiveness your cross?

D'Ambrosio, Marcellino. *Jesus the Way, the Truth, and the Life*, Ascension, 2020, pp. 214.

US Catholic Church. *Catechism of the Catholic Church: Complete and Updated,* Crown Publishing, 1995, pp.404.

41. Leave "if only" behind

Escriva, St. Josemaria. *Conversations with Monsignor Escriva de Balanger*, Scepter Publishers, 2008.

Trudeau, Margaret. *Changing my Mind*, HarperCollins, 2011.

42. Is connection on your "have a good day" checklist?

Neves, Antonio. *Stop Living on Autopilot: Take Responsibility for your Life and Rediscover a Bolder, Happier You*, Harmony/Rodale, 2021.

43. When it feels like He's not there

"I Have Called You By Name." *Chosen*, created by Dallas Jenkins, season 1, episode 1, Loaves & Fishes Productions / Angel Studios / Out of Order Studios, 21 April 2019. *Amazon Prime*, primevideo.com.

Ocariz, Father Fernando. "Felicitacion de Navidad del prelado del Opus Dei." Prelature of Opus Dei YouTube channel, 2021, Spanish with English subtitles, https://youtu.be/IdCyyt9TTiQ.

44. Holiness is a lifelong journey

Letters to Myself from the End of the World, created by Emily Stimson Chapman and Fr. Dave Pivonka, Wild Goose TV, 2018, https://thewildgooseisloose.com/letters.

Lewis, C.S. *The Chronicles of Narnia 7-Book Box Set*, HarperCollins, 2002.

Hallow: Prayer and Meditation (app), Hallow Inc.,Version 8.0.1, 2022, https://hallow.com/features/.

Tolkien, J.R.R. *The Lord of the Rings*, HarperCollins, 1991.

45. A fresh perspective

Chapman, Emily Stimpson. *Letters to Myself from the End of the World*, Emmaus Road Publishing, 2021, pp.59.

Chase, Aimee. *Present not Perfect: A Journal for Slowing Down, Letting Go and Loving Who You Are*, St. Martin's Publishing Group, 2017, pp. 125.

46. A chef's healing cooking

Saint Pope John Paul II. *Encyclical Letter Ecclesia de Eucharistia*, 14 April 2003, https://www.vatican.va/content/john-paul-ii/en/encyclicals/documents/hf_jp-ii_enc_20030417_eccl-de-euch.html.

47. Inspired by an Italian pianist and composer

Giurioli, Alberto. "Following Yourself." Alberto Giurioli's YouTube channel, 3 September 2017, https://youtu.be/69icErBHi7c.

Giurioli, Alberto. "Tutto e bellissimo." Alberto Giurioli's YouTube channel, 8 October 2019, https://youtu.be/gagpxWxsduU.

Myra, Harold and Brother Lawrence. *The Practice of God: Experience the Spiritual Classic Through 40 Days of Daily Devotion*, E-book ed., Discovery House Publishers, 2017, pp. 21.

48. God delights in you through all your troubles

Feucht, Sean. "You delight in me." *The Things We Did at First*, Sean Feucht's YouTube channel, 24 April 2022, https://youtu.be/5J5Ea6tSm1o.

49. Even in adversity there can be joy

Sheen, Venerable Fulton. *Way to Happiness: An Inspiring Guide to Peace, Hope and Contentment*, Alba House, 1997, pp. 24.

Kreeft, Peter. *Heaven, the Heart's Deepest Longing*, Ignatius Press, 1989, pp. 52.

Houselander, Caryll. *The Reed of God*, Ave Maria Press, 2006, pp. 31.

50. The bravest thing you can do is ask for help

B.C. Catholic. Published by the Archdiocese of Vancouver. https://bccatholic.ca/.

Brown, Brené. [@BrenéBrown]. "Asking for help is one of the bravest things we'll ever do. #BellLetsTalk." *Twitter*, Jan 27, 2016, https://twitter.com/brenebrown/status/692394692684574720?lang=ca.

Dawson, Devin. "I Got a Truck." Devin Dawson's YouTube channel, 2 Sep 2020, https://youtu.be/8UznHJ6hIvA.

Lewis, C.S. *Till We Have Faces: A Myth Retold*, HarperOne, Reissue edition, 2017, pp. 111.

Resources

Helplines, Courses and Counsellors

1-800-784-2433: 24-hour line for individuals with thoughts of suicide.

310-6789: For individuals who need emotional support. No area code required.

Vancouver, Canada, faith-based Mental Health Ministry: https://sanctuarymentalhealth.org/

The Sanctuary Course for Catholics: https://sanctuarymentalhealth.org/catholics/ (Lisa shares her story in the fourth video on Companionship)

Science based and Christ-centred resources: https://mentalhealthgracealliance.org/your-personal-journey

Chicago Diocese, Mental Illness Ministry: http://www.miministry.org/prayer.htm

Website for Catholic Counsellors in the Vancouver Archdiocese: https://rcav.org/personal-counselling

About the Author

Lisa Rumpel is a writer, speaker, and host of *The Will to Thrive Podcast; Stories of Resilience*. Born in Vancouver, British Columbia, Lisa has crafted stories since she was a little girl and studied creative writing at Kwantlen Polytechnic University.

In 2019, Lisa received a Canadian Christian Communicators award for her column in the *BC Catholic Newspaper*. She has been a guest on CBC Radio's *On the Coast Show* with Gloria Macarenko to discuss mental health and the Catholic Church. She also shares her story in the *Sanctuary Course for Catholics* produced by Sanctuary Mental Health Ministries. You can find the video course here: https://sanctuarymentalhealth.org/catholics/.

During the week Lisa can be found working in an office. She enjoys good coffee, reading, and dancing like no one is watching. She lives in Vancouver, her favourite rainforest.

Connect with Lisa:

Website: https://resilientcatholic.home.blog/

Instagram: https://www.instagram.com/resilientlisa/

B.C. Catholic Newspaper: https://bccatholic.ca/authors/lisa-rumpel

Podcast: The Will to Thrive: Stories of Resilience: https://anchor.fm/lisa-rumpel (also available on your favorite podcast platform)

Manufactured by Amazon.ca
Bolton, ON